WHY JOHNNY
CAN'T PREACH

WHY JOHNNY CAN'T PREACH

The Media Have Shaped the Messengers

T. DAVID GORDON

P.O. BOX 817 • PHILLIPSBURG • NEW JERSEY 08865-0817

Printed in the United States of America

Library of Congress Cataloging-in-Publication Data

Gordon, T. David, 1954–
  Why Johnny can't preach : the media have shaped the messengers / T. David Gordon.
      p. cm.
  Includes bibliographical references.
  ISBN 978-1-59638-116-2 (pbk.)
  1. Mass media in religion. 2. Mass media—Influence. 3. Preaching. I. Title.
  BV652.95.G63 2009
  251—dc22
                          2008048517

This book is dedicated to

David F. Wells

on the occasion of his retirement from theological education.
He is recognized by the public for his remarkable learning,
intelligence, and insight; his friends are privileged to have
also benefited from his compassion and wisdom.

CONTENTS

PREFACE

WITH THE EXCEPTION of a few revisions, I wrote this book in 2004, while I was undergoing eleven months of treatment for cancer. The book contains a few references to that situation, and I have chosen to leave them there because without the cancer, the book would probably not have been written. I had stage III colorectal cancer, and the various cancer Web sites at the time gave me a 25 percent chance of survival. I'm not a mathematician, but I realized that those numbers were not very encouraging, and I had to face the realistic possibility that I would not survive the year. Having been concerned about the state of preaching for three decades, I believed that it would be irresponsible to leave the world without expressing my thoughts about the matter, in the hope that better preaching might be the result.

Such circumstances may not justify the writing of such a book, but I hope that they at least explain it. Dr. Samuel Johnson is reported to have said: "Depend upon it, Sir, when a man knows he is to be hanged in a fortnight, it concentrates his mind wonderfully." My cancer concentrated my mind wonderfully also. The manuscript is therefore, at a minimum, heartfelt.

Perhaps I should have stated the matter less directly (or titled the book less impishly), but the cancer only concentrated my mind; it did not necessarily lighten my attitude. The project took on a sense of urgency, and I have chosen to preserve that tone in the manuscript rather than rewrite the entire thing in such a manner as to blunt its force. Charitable readers will, I trust, forgive me (and concerned readers should know that I remain in remission to date).

I believed then, and believe now, that the profound shifts in dominant media in the last half of the twentieth century have profoundly misshaped the sensibilities of the typical American, and that this, in turn, has led to a profound decline in preaching. What follows is a partial explanation for the decline in preaching over the last half century, with a few suggestions for its remedy. It is not the full story, and it does not intend to be the full story. But as someone who teaches media ecology, I realize that I have a somewhat distinctive point of view on the matter, one that I believe warrants the public's attention.

As a matter of style, I have abandoned any attempt to find a gender neutral third person pronoun. I tire of the stylistically awkward "he/she" and "him/her," so I continue to employ the older practice of using the masculine pronoun generically. It is not my intention thereby to exclude females; readers may substitute generic feminine pronouns if they prefer them.

INTRODUCTION

I'VE WANTED TO WRITE about certain things for many years—things that I have not yet written because I haven't had the schedule necessary to do the job well. But one other thing I've wanted to write for at least twenty years has been delayed for an entirely different reason: I fear that those who have ministered and preached to me will assume I am talking about them and become discouraged. I've always feared to state publicly that, in my opinion, less than 30 percent of those who are ordained to the Christian ministry can preach an even mediocre sermon, lest I appear to be ungrateful or uncharitable. On the other hand, to sit in the kettle as it rises degree by degree toward the boiling point, while doing nothing to alert others, concerns me also. I've finally, therefore, determined to go ahead and record my thoughts on the matter, so that I can satisfy my conscience. But let me just state from the outset that what I say about preaching is generally true of preaching in North America in the twenty-first century; it is not merely peculiar to my own experience in the particular individual churches of which I've been a member. Sometimes I have been under ministry that is the exception to the ordinary cultural pattern; sometimes I have not—but I do not intend for anyone to try to guess which were which.

The only sense in which this book is written about my own particular experience is that, in my adult years, I have "run" in conservative evangelical and conservative Reformed churches. I taught at a conservative evangelical seminary, Gordon-Conwell Theological Seminary in Massachusetts, and my wife and I, through thirty years of marriage, have ordinarily been members of Presbyterian Church in America and Orthodox Presbyterian churches. Therefore, I am unqualified to state anecdotally that the patterns I have observed are broader than this. For all I know personally, the typical Lutheran pulpit is healthy today; and the mainline Methodists are preaching along beautifully. But since I argue that the *causes* for the impoverished conservative evangelical and Reformed pulpit are largely the cultural changes in the second half of the twentieth century, I'd be surprised if other communions were immune from that which I lament. At any rate, I don't intend to throw stones at others; it is the conservative evangelical churches and conservative Reformed churches with which I am primarily acquainted. If others perceive similar tendencies in their own communions, then I hope some of the proposed remedies will be helpful there also.[1]

1. If anything, my experience with the mainline Presbyterian churches (PCUSA) has been somewhat different from my experience in the more conservative Reformed churches (OPC and PCA). Preaching in the mainline Presbyterian churches is ordinarily better crafted than it is in the conservative Reformed churches, but its content is not predictably orthodox in any historically Christian sense. In the more conservative churches, the content (insofar as it is discernible, and it isn't always) is more reminiscent of historic Christianity, but the craftsmanship is ordinarily poor. So for

Further, if what I say appears uncharitable or ungrateful, forgive me, and try to understand my circumstances. As I write this, I have completed one of three fairly severe phases of treatment for a stage III cancer. My prognosis is improving, and I may live some more years, possibly even another decade or two. But as I have lain awake many nights over the last three months, I have been forced to ask what I have done—and, worse, what I haven't done—and I have simply become persuaded that my silence on such an important matter borders on the irresponsible. Before I die, I must express my opinion on this subject. If the opinion is wrong, fine; dismiss it as wrongheaded. But I can fulfill my duty only by declaring my mind (right or wrong) on this important matter.

As you will see from what follows, while there is always some subjective element in the assessment of preaching, I will present evidence that goes beyond this. I am not evaluating preaching by some peculiar, idiosyncratic definition, nor (in this place) do I intend to articulate my views on some of the valid debates within the sphere of homiletics (such as how to preach Christ from Old Testament texts). That is, I am talking about Christian preaching only in its generic sense, and the standards by which I evaluate preaching are universal in the sense that no one has ever argued for the alternative. For example, I will argue that few sermons have unity, and that

American Presbyterians, our options are ordinarily either a well-prepared sermon that isn't distinctively Christian or a Christian sermon that we cannot follow, neither of which strikes me as much of a bargain. Further, in neither pulpit is the preaching particularly significant. In each, our culture's Cult of the Insignificant has triumphed over an earlier generation's Cult of the Significant.

the lack of unity is a serious, if not fatal, defect in a sermon. Has anyone argued for disunity in preaching? Has any notable homiletical textbook in the history of the church encouraged disunity? Or again, most sermons have no recognizable order to them, no apparent rationale for why the first point precedes the second; yet has anyone ever argued for disorganized preaching, or suggested that it is a homiletical virtue to simply articulate a number of disordered observations randomly occasioned by reading the text? Of course not. As we will see in chapter 1 in evaluating Robert Lewis Dabney's seven "cardinal requisites" of a sermon, that list contains nothing idiosyncratic. And yet one rarely hears a sermon today with all seven, and I have heard many sermons without *any* of the seven.

Further, I wish to clarify that I do *not* mean what ministers wrongly and defensively assume I mean: that we do not have many *great* preachers in our day. In an effort at deflecting the weight of my observation, many ministers attempt to agree with a distortion of my concern: "Ah, David, you're right; ours is not a day of great preaching." This is not my concern. First, I'm not sure there ever *was* any great preaching (much of what others consider to be great I find to be defective); and second, I don't care about its presence or absence one whit. What I care about is the *average* Christian family in the *average* pew in the *average* church on the *average* Sunday. And the problem there is not that we don't have "great" preachers; in many circumstances we don't even have mediocre preachers. If Jesus tests Peter's profession of love by the ministerial act of feeding his sheep, our sheep do not need gourmet meals.

But they do need good, solid nourishment, and they are not ordinarily getting it.

And finally, as the title suggests, the problem is not primarily due to laziness or defensiveness (though the latter is a serious problem; ministers as a group are more resistant to annual review and constructive criticism than any other profession of my acquaintance). Rather, I will suggest that *societal* changes that led to the concerns expressed in the 1960s to 1980s in educational circles—societal changes reflected in a decline in the ability to read (texts) and write—have led to the natural cultural consequence that people cannot preach expositorily. This is why I self-consciously title this book after the *Why Johnny Can't Read* and *Why Johnny Can't Write* books of that period.[2] Thus, the solution (insofar as I offer one) is not to demonize the poor preachers or to encourage them to work harder, nor is it to blame the theological seminaries; the solution will require some understanding of how shifts in culturally dominant media alter not only the social environment, but the individual's sensibilities also.

This short book is subtitled *The Media Have Shaped the Messengers*. Media ecology is not yet well known as an academic discipline, nor is it especially well known as a subset of culture analysis. It does exist, however, and I teach an introduction to

2. Rudolf Flesch, *Why Johnny Can't Read: And What You Can Do about It* (New York: Harper, 1966); Myra J. Linden and Arthur Whimbey, *Why Johnny Can't Write: How to Improve Writing Skills* (Hillsdale, NJ: Lawrence Erlbaum Associates, 1990). The titles of these works also explain the *Johnny* in my title. *Johnny* was then generic, referring to both males and females, and I have adopted the generic term for my title also, because I fear that "Jane" is no freer from the cultural influences I mention than is "Johnny."

media ecology at the college level, and have been influenced by its prominent contributors, such as Socrates (who questioned the value of writing), Marshall McLuhan, Walter Ong, Jacques Ellul, and Neil Postman. Postman coined the term *media ecology* to describe how changes in dominant media alter the human and social *environment*. Media ecology, as a discipline, is comparatively less concerned with the content of a given medium and more concerned about how the mere presence of that medium itself alters individual consciousness, social structures, or cultural habits and sensibilities. In this book, I am asking a media-ecological question: How has the movement from language-based media to image-based and electronic media altered our sensibilities, and how, in turn, has this change in sensibility shaped today's preachers? I will suggest, at the proper point, that exposition of a text, whether sacred or secular, requires the development of certain human sensibilities which, if not developed, render the individual as incapable of preaching as if he had no larynx. But first, let me attempt to establish my thesis: that many ordained people simply can't preach.

I

JOHNNY CAN'T PREACH

PART OF ME WISHES to avoid proving the sordid truth: that preaching today is ordinarily poor. But I have come to recognize that many, many individuals today have never been under a steady diet of competent preaching. As a consequence, they are satisfied with what they hear because they have nothing better with which to compare it. Therefore, for many individuals, the kettle in which they live has always been at the boiling point, and they've simply adjusted to it. As starving children in Manila sift through the landfill for food, Christians in many churches today have never experienced genuinely soul-nourishing preaching, and so they just pick away at what is available to them, trying to find a morsel of spiritual sustenance or helpful counsel here or there. So let me provide just some of the lines of evidence that have persuaded me that preaching today is in substantial disarray.

Anecdotal Evidence

I candidly admit that one line of evidence is subjective and anecdotal. For twenty-five years or more, I routinely have found myself asking my wife, "What was that sermon about?"—to which she has responded: "I'm not really sure." And when we have both been able to discern *what* the sermon was about, I have then asked: "Do you think it was responsibly based on the text read?" and the answer has ordinarily been negative (matching my own opinion that the point of the message was entirely unsatisfactory). I would guess that of the sermons I've heard in the last twenty-five years, 15 percent had a discernible point; I could say, "The sermon was about X." Of those 15 percent, however, less than 10 percent demonstrably based the point on the text read. That is, no competent effort was made to persuade the hearer that God's Word required a particular thing; it was simply asserted.[1]

Such sermons are religiously useless. If the hearer's duty in listening to a sermon is to be willing to submit one's will to God's will, then one can only do this if the preacher does *his* duty of demonstrating that what he is saying *is* God's will. When the Westminster Confession refers to the "conscionable hearing" of the Word, this is what it means—to hear it as an act of conscience, which is bound to obey God.

---

1. Nor am I alone here. At a faculty meeting at Gordon-Conwell once, someone reported that a study had disclosed that one-half of ordained ministers leave the profession before retiring. Most of the faculty gasped at this, but my good colleague Doug Stuart remarked: "I wish the number were higher; only about one in five can preach."

But the conscience is *not* bound to obey the minister; the minister is only to be obeyed insofar as he *demonstrates* to the hearer what *God's* will is. Therefore, there is no religious use (in the Protestant and Reformed sense; I am not qualified to speak about homilies in the Roman Catholic tradition) in a sermon that merely discloses the *minister's* opinion, but does not disclose the opinion of God. And there surely can be no use in a sermon that does not even disclose the minister's opinion clearly.

I've really desired something fairly simple for my family: to be able to talk intelligently about the sermon on Sunday afternoon or throughout the week. And to do this, all I really desire is the ability to answer three questions: What was the point or thrust of the sermon? Was this point adequately established in the text that was read? Were the applications legitimate applications of the point, from which we can have further fruitful conversation about other possible applications? Frequently, indeed more commonly than not, I have heard sermons about which my family cannot even answer the first question. And even when we can, it is very rare to find the point adequately established from the passage. Further, the applications suggested almost never have anything to do with the text. I find myself forced to concur with the judgment of Benjamin Franklin, who once heard a Presbyterian minister's sermon and afterward remarked:

> At length he took for his Text that Verse of the 4th Chapter of Philippians, *Finally, Brethren, Whatsoever Things are true, honest, just, pure, lovely, or of good report, if there be any virtue, or any praise,*

think on these Things; and I imagin'd in a Sermon on such a Text,
we could not miss of having some Morality: But he confin'd
himself to five Points only as meant by the Apostle, viz. I.
Keeping holy the Sabbath Day. 2. Being diligent in Reading
the Holy Scriptures. 3. Attending duly the Public Worship.
4. Partaking of the Sacrament. 5. Paying a due Respect to
God's Ministers.—These might be all good Things, but as
they were not the kind of good Things that I expected from
that Text, I despaired of ever meeting them from any other,
was disgusted, and attended his Preaching no more.[2]

Like Franklin, I find myself somewhat "disgusted" with
sermons for the same reason he was. Unlike the deistic Franklin, however, I don't consider myself free simply to not attend
church on Sunday, so his solution doesn't work for me and my
family. Nor is my experience or Franklin's unusual. I find that
others have noted the same kinds of defects in preaching.

2. *The Autobiography of Benjamin Franklin*, ed. Leonard W. Labaree et al. (New
Haven: Yale University Press, 1964), 147–48. Franklin's comments should not
be dismissed due to religious prejudice, despite his objections to many Christian
doctrines, and to the Calvinist/Presbyterian doctrines particularly (ibid., 146).
Franklin appreciated George Whitefield's oratory, writing approvingly of his (Cal-
vinist/Presbyterian) preaching, which moved Franklin to unexpected pecuniary
support: "I happened soon after to attend one of his Sermons, in the Course of
which I perceived he intended to finish with a Collection, and I silently resolved
he should get nothing from me. I had in my Pocket a Handful of Copper Money,
three or four silver Dollars, and five Pistoles in Gold. As he proceeded I began
to soften, and concluded to give the Coppers. Another Stroke of his Oratory
made me asham'd of that, and determin'd me to give the Silver; and he finish'd so
admirably, that I empty'd my Pocket wholly into the Collector's Dish, Gold and
all" (ibid., 177). Cf. also the summary of the surprisingly cooperative relationship
between Franklin and Whitefield in Walter Isaacson, *Benjamin Franklin: An American
Life* (New York: Simon and Schuster, 2003), 110–13.

The Testimony of a Ruling-Elder Rotarian

Roughly twenty-five years ago, when the matter of ineffective preaching was initially beginning to concern me, I spoke with a ruling elder who was active in the presbytery of which I was then a part. When a church in that presbytery called a certain minister, I asked this particular elder (after I had heard the minister preach) why they had hired a man who didn't appear to be able to preach. The elder in question was known by all to be one of the most charitable, compassionate men in the entire presbytery, so I was stunned by his answer: "David, of course he can't preach; but I've served on pulpit committees off and on for thirty years, and nobody can preach. We just look for men who are gifted in other areas, and who are orthodox, but we accept from the outset of the search that we are not likely to find a person who can preach." He continued: "You know, as a businessman, I've been in Rotary for almost thirty years, and every month we have a meeting and someone gives a talk of some sort. When I go home, I can tell my wife what the talk was about, and how the person made his point. But I can rarely do that with sermons. I think we should shut the theological seminaries down, and send our candidates to Rotary International." Now, this elder was not some old crank. He was the most upbeat, Christlike, compassionate man I knew, and he was not negative or combative by nature. Further, he admitted that there were exceptions: Richard Pratt (now a professor at Reformed Theological Seminary in Orlando) was a licentiate in the presbytery at that time, and this elder said: "Now, Richard—he *can* preach." And he was right; Richard can indeed preach. But the conversation with the elder was disturbing because it encouraged me to believe that my own observations were correct: that preaching has become seriously, seriously defective.[3]

The Common (Almost Universal) Evaluation of Ministers by Their Congregations

My anecdotal observation about the nature of preaching today has also been reinforced perhaps a hundred times by casual conversations I have had with people whom I meet. If they are churched, I ask them where they live, where they go to church, and whether they are happy with their church. They ordinarily say that they are. But then I ask: "What do you think of your minister?" Most of the time, the reply I get is: "Well, he's not a great preacher, but . . ." That is, almost everywhere I go, when I ask people about their church home, they almost universally say that their minister is "not a great preacher," which we all know is just a polite way of saying that he's a poor preacher. It's a kind and charitable way of saying: "Well, we don't really benefit from his preaching, but he's a very good minister in other ways." And while I'm delighted to hear that ministers are faithful in visitation, compassionate in caring for the sick, efficient in administration, or winsome

3. Less than two years later, another ruling elder in the same presbytery told me virtually the same thing: that he had served on several pulpit committees through the years, and he just accepted it as a given that they would not find a man who could preach, so they simply looked for candidates who could do other things well.

toward the youth or the lost, I'd be even more delighted to hear *someone* say the opposite: "Well, he's a little awkward at visitation, but he is outstanding in the pulpit; and the preaching is so good, and so nourishing, that we put up with the other minor defects in other areas."

Dabney's "Cardinal Requisites" Are Manifestly Absent

For those who remain unconvinced, I call attention to Robert Lewis Dabney's *Lectures on Sacred Rhetoric.*[4] This became a standard text on homiletics in the late nineteenth century, and it was well reviewed not only by Presbyterian journals, but by Episcopal, Methodist, and Baptist sources as well. There was nothing idiosyncratic in it (though there were several idiosyncrasies in Dabney's other writings), and while his thorough study of ancient rhetoric is off-putting to contemporary readers, no one would take exception to the two chapters in which he enumerates "The Seven Cardinal Requisites of Preaching." These seven requisites (not excellences, but requisites) are seven minimal requirements that Dabney believed (and his reviewers agreed) were essential to every sermon. None of these seven categories is subjective; each is perfectly susceptible of objective evaluation.[5] Here is his list,

4. Robert Lewis Dabney, *Sacred Rhetoric: or a Course of Lectures on Preaching* (Richmond: Presbyterian Committee of Publication, 1870; repr., Edinburgh: Banner of Truth, 1979).

5. The third requisite, "evangelical tone," may appear to be subjective, and a matter merely of style. But as will be seen in chapter 4 on the content of preaching, what Dabney meant by this is the dominating, controlling soteric and Christological focus of every sermon.

briefly articulated; those interested in reading his own lengthier descriptions may read the entirety of his chapters.

1. Textual Fidelity

Here Dabney's Protestantism is visible. For Dabney, a minister is an ambassador, who represents another, declaring the will of that Other. Therefore, he is not entitled to preach his own insights, his own opinions, or even his own settled convictions; he is entitled only to declare the mind of God revealed in Holy Scripture. Since the mind of God is disclosed in Scripture, the sermon must be entirely faithful to the text—a genuine exposition of the particular thought of the particular text.

Test: Does the significant point of the sermon arise out of the significant point of the text? Is the thrust of the sermon merely an aside in the text? Is the text merely a pretext for the minister's own idea?

2. Unity

"Unity requires these two things. The speaker must, first, have one main subject of discourse, to which he adheres with supreme reference throughout. But this is not enough. He must, second, propose to himself one definite impression on the hearer's soul, to the making of which everything in the sermon is bent."[6]

Test: If ten people are asked after the sermon what the sermon was about, will at least eight of them give the same (or a similar) answer?

6. Dabney, *Sacred Rhetoric,* 109.

3. Evangelical Tone

"It is defined by Vinet as 'the general savour of Christianity, a gravity accompanied by tenderness, a severity tempered with sweetness, a majesty associated with intimacy.' Blair calls it 'gravity and warmth united' . . . an ardent zeal for God's glory and a tender compassion for those who are perishing."[7]

Test: Do hearers get the impression that the minister is *for* them (eager to see them richly blessed by a gracious God), or *against* them (eager to put them in their place, scold them, reprimand them, or punish them)? Is it his desire to see them reconciled to and blessed by a pardoning God? Does the sermon press the hearer to consider the hopelessness of his condition apart from Christ, and the utter competence of Christ to rescue the penitent sinner?

4. Instructiveness

The instructive sermon is that which abounds in food for the understanding. It is full of thought, and richly informs the mind of the hearer. It is opposed, of course, to vapid and commonplace compositions; but it is opposed also to those which seek to reach the will through rhetorical ornament and passionate sentiment, without establishing rational conviction. . . . Religion is an intelligent concern, and deals with man as a reasoning creature. Sanctification is by the truth. To move men we must instruct. No Christian can be stable and consistent save as he is intelligent. . . . If you would not wear out after you have ceased to be a novelty, give the minds of your people food.[8]

7. Ibid., 116–17.
8. Ibid., 117–19.

Test: Does the sermon significantly engage the mind, or is the sermon full of commonplace clichés, slogans, and general truths? Is the hearer genuinely likely to rethink his view of God, society, church, or self, or his reasons for holding his current views? Is the mind of the attentive listener engaged or repulsed?

5. Movement

Movement is not a blow or shock, communicating only a single or instantaneous impulse, but a sustained progress. It is, in short, that force thrown from the soul of the orator into his discourse, by which the soul of the hearer is urged, with a constant and accelerated progress, toward that practical impression which is designed for the result. . . . The language of the orator must possess, in all its flow, a nervous brevity and a certain well-ordered haste, like that of the racer pressing to his goal.[9]

Test: Do the earlier parts of the sermon contribute to the latter parts' full effect? Does the address have intellectual (and consequently emotional) momentum?

6. Point

Dabney uses the word *point* to describe the overall intellectual and emotional impact of a sermon. Point is thus a result of unity, movement, and order, which put a convincing, compelling weight on the soul of the hearer. The hearer feels a certain

9. Ibid., 122–24.

point impressing itself on him, and feels that he must either agree or disagree, assent or deny.

Test: Is the effect of the sermon, on those who believe it, similar? If it encouraged one, did it tend to encourage all, and for the same reason? If it troubled one, did it tend to trouble all, and for the same reason? If it made one thankful, did it tend to make all thankful, and for the same reason?

7. *Order*

We would probably call this *organization*, but the idea is the same. A discourse (sacred or otherwise) cannot have unity, movement, or point without having order. Order is simply the proper *arrangement* of the parts, so that what is earlier prepares for what is later. A well-ordered sermon reveals a sermon's unity, makes the sermon memorable, and gives the sermon great point.

Test: Could the hearers compare notes and reproduce the outline of the sermon? If they could not reproduce the outline, could they state how it progressed from one part to another?

I don't insist that Dabney's way of describing what is essential to a sermon is the only, or necessarily best, way of doing so. One could make a reasonable case that both movement and point are in fact results of a sermon that has unity and is well ordered. We would then be left with five essential traits of a Christian sermon: that it have unity and order, and that it be expositional, evangelical (i.e., Christ-centered), and instructive. I don't think anyone could argue against these, and I don't believe, in homiletical history, that anyone ever *has* argued against them. Some have rightly complained that a sermon can be instructive in the wrong *way*: delivered as a lecture, and filled with far too much information and far too little wisdom, insight, or understanding. But I don't believe anyone has ever argued that a sermon should not be instructive in the sense that Dabney meant it, that it appealed *to* the entire human *through* the mind or understanding.

Yet Dabney's seven cardinal requisites today are honored almost exclusively in their breach. Sermons rarely have unity, are rarely based on a responsible exposition of the text, are almost never instructive (except in the sense of dropping the occasional tidbit of data that wasn't known to the entire congregation before), and have little discernible order. To rehearse Dabney's list of seven is to expose the present defective nature of preaching, because most of us know that we rarely, if ever, hear a sermon with all seven of these qualities, or even my abbreviated five.

The Almost Universal Desire for Briefer Sermons

This point is closely related to what I say below about the annual review, but it is a distinct matter to be considered in its own right. When something is well done, we do not complain about its length. A group of us went to Heinz Hall in Pittsburgh several years ago to hear André Previn conduct the Brahms *Ein Deutsches Requiem*. When the performance ended, there was a hush over the audience, as the final bars of triple piano in the chorus whispered the closing movement to a restive end. Time passed before the applause began, because the entire audience had been mesmerized by the outstanding performance of this great work. No one wanted to leave ten minutes earlier, nor were people checking their watches ten minutes before the conclusion. All of us would have happily stayed for another half hour of such a performance, and we were saddened that it had ended. When we experience a thing that is well done, we get caught up in it, become lost in the moment, and lose any sense of the passage of time. When a public speaker has something important to say, and says it in a well-organized manner that enables the audience to perceive its significance, the reaction is similar. People do not look at their watches, clear their throats, stretch, and do a number of other nervous exercises indicative of their boredom. But if that public discourse is listless, rambling, disorganized, without clear purpose, and uninspiring, ten minutes seems like an eternity.

This is also true of speeches that are more private, such as those given by a genuinely talented conversationalist or a professional explaining a service. When my wife and I visited a surgeon to discuss what to do about my cancer, he spoke to us for what we would later realize was close to forty-five minutes, but in the entire time neither my wife nor I checked our watches to see when he might stop. We had a profound interest in my cancer and in its treatment, and we listened attentively to a well-organized, informative, and sensitively delivered discussion about the cancer, its treatment, and my prognosis (unhappily, about 25 percent). We would have complained about the length of the meeting had the surgeon been unclear, disorganized, cliché-ridden, or uninterested. Therefore, I suggest that it is not the case (as is so often argued) that people have a reduced attention span today, and that this is why they object to the length of the sermons. People may very well have a reduced attention span, but even so, they have no difficulty giving attention to a discourse they deem important and well organized. Bad preaching is insufferably long, even if the chronological length is brief.

Ask the average churchgoer if he wishes his minister would preach a little longer or a little briefer, and nearly everyone will say, "A little [or a lot] briefer." Indeed, once when I lived in a town not known for having any particularly able preachers, a friend who attended another church suggested that his preacher was the best in the area. Having heard nothing to suggest that this preacher was especially able, I probed further and asked my friend the basis for his conclusion. He answered: "Well, no one within half an hour of here can preach, but George [name altered to protect] at least *knows* he can't preach, so he preaches very briefly. All the others, who can't hold your attention for ten minutes, drone on for thirty or forty. George only holds you hostage to the limit of your tolerance." Now, this was damning with faint praise, to be sure, but it is further evidence of the current state of preaching. It is often so bad that the best we can say about some preachers is that they themselves realize it, and are merciful in the length of their sermons. By contrast, I've heard ministers whose sermons I was disappointed to have come to an end. These entire sermons had been so well delivered—so thoughtful, so faithful to the text without being pedantic, so insightful without being idiosyncratic, so well organized as to appear seamless, so challenging and nourishing to my soul—that I just didn't want the experience to end. I realized then that sermon length is not measured in minutes; it is measured in minutes-beyond-interest, in the amount of time the minister continues to preach after he has lost the interest of his hearers (assuming he ever kindled it in the first place).

Ministers have found it entirely too convenient and self-serving to dismiss congregational disinterest on the basis of attenuated attention spans or spiritual indifference. In most cases, the inattentiveness in the congregation is due to poor preaching—preaching that does not reward an energetic, conscientious listening. When attentive listeners are not rewarded for their energetic attentiveness, they eventually become inattentive.

The Contemporary and Emergent Churches

In some cases, there is no difference between churches that adopt so-called contemporary worship and those that call themselves "emergent" or "emerging." It is also possible, I suppose, to be one without the other. One common trait among them is their conviction that the church's liturgical practices need to be jettisoned and replaced with something else. A common basis for this contention is the claim that most, if not all, traditional churches are moribund and irrelevant. While I think this claim is exaggerated, I don't think it is entirely false. Some churches, perhaps a good many, are indeed moribund. What the contemporaneists and emergents have not yet considered, however, is the possibility that such moribund churches are so

31

not because they are doing the wrong things, but because they are doing them incompetently.

The Westminster Shorter Catechism's 89th answer says this: "The Spirit of God maketh the reading, but especially the preaching, of the Word, an effectual means of convincing and converting sinners, and of building them up in holiness and comfort, through faith, unto salvation." Now, what would the church want to do other than convince and convert sinners, and build them up in holiness and comfort unto salvation? But is everything that is called *preaching* true preaching, as Westminster understood preaching? Is there sacramental power to merely making utterances behind a pulpit? Not according to the Westminster Directory for Worship, which lists a number of specific requirements of preaching. So if the church is not effectual in convincing, converting, and comforting sinners, is it because preaching will not accomplish this, or because the preaching is poorly done?[10]

I believe the preaching in many churches is so poorly done that it is not, effectively, preaching. The contemporaneists and emergents implicitly deny what Westminster says about preaching, and so they attempt to achieve the church's ends through other means. I concur with them that the church is failing in many circumstances, but I attribute this not to

10. Several of the more incompetent preachers I've heard have jumped on the emergent bandwagon, and their ministerial careers are undergoing a resurgence now, as people flock to hear their enthusiastic worship leaders and to ogle their PowerPoint presentations. Their churches are no longer moribund, but then the annual carnival isn't, either—it, too, is full of enthusiasm, activity, and lively entertainment. But I'm not sure these emergent activities have any more spiritual effect than the pig races at the carnival.

the church's employing the wrong means, but to the church's employing the right means incompetently. If the patients of a given hospital's surgeons continue to die, we could, I suppose, abandon the scalpel. We might also consider employing it more skillfully. My challenge to the contemporaneists and emergents is this: Show me a church where the preaching is good, and yet the church is still moribund. I've never seen such a church. The moribund churches I've seen have been malpreached to death. But the fact that large segments of the church are abandoning anything like traditional preaching altogether establishes my point: that Johnny can't preach. He preaches so poorly that even believers have come to disbelieve that God has chosen through the folly of preaching to save those who believe (1 Cor. 1:21).

The Annual Review

My final argument to prove that preaching is in bad shape today is the annual review—or, to be more exact, its absence. Almost no churches conduct an annual review of the pastoral staff. When I took my church in New Hampshire years ago, it had not been their practice either. So during the contract negotiation stage, I asked them to pay me less than they had proposed, but to give me two things in return: a week of study leave, and an annual review. I did this because I believe it is absolutely essential for any professional to have an annual review of his labor. Those of us who teach are reviewed; those who work in business are reviewed. Every other realm of labor recognizes the importance of an annual review, in which strengths and weaknesses can be assessed as a means to more fruitful service in the future.

So why don't churches routinely conduct annual reviews of their ministers? Because ministers don't want to be told that their preaching is disorganized, hard to follow, irrelevant, and poorly reasoned; and because churches don't want to insult their ministers or hurt their feelings (and churches often know that the review would have some negative aspects). Therefore, I suggest that the very absence of annual reviews stands as glaring proof that preaching is so bad today that no one—neither the preacher nor the hearer—can tolerate the thought of how painful it would be to provide an honest assessment.

Are the Seminaries at Fault?

Typically, at this point on a topic such as this, we begin blaming the seminaries. I taught at Gordon-Conwell Seminary for thirteen years, and have guest-lectured at several others, so I know firsthand that theological education is imperfect. Bad preaching today, however, is not the result of the failure of the seminaries. In fact, some seminaries are doing excellent work in homiletics, and some very skilled people are involved in its instruction. I might mention several such examples: Gordon-Conwell's Haddon Robinson (with his colleague Scott Gibson) is a fine preacher and a fine teacher of preachers who has written an excellent book on expository preaching. President Bryan Chapell of Covenant Theological Seminary has also written a fine book on preaching, is himself an outstanding preacher, and teaches preaching effectively. President Bill Carl of Pittsburgh

Theological Seminary is a fine preacher and homiletician, as is his almost-neighbor Paul Zahl, dean of Trinity Episcopal School for Ministry. And President Joseph Pipa of Greenville Seminary is a very fine preacher, who along with these others (and many others) is a fine instructor in homiletics. This list could continue because, if anything, we have an embarrassment of riches among homileticians at seminaries today.

The problem is the condition of the typical ministerial candidate when he *arrives* at seminary. The culture has profoundly changed since the 1950s. A culture formerly dominated by language (reading and writing) has become a culture dominated by images, even moving images. Not only television and film, but also magazines and newspapers have become much more image-based than they were in the 1950s. *Life* and *Look* magazines spent enormous sums in the 1960s hiring first-rate photographers to produce magazines for general consumption that were primarily about their pictures; and the text merely accompanied a story told primarily by photographs. As the late Librarian of Congress Daniel Boorstin said: "Photography was destined soon to give printed matter itself a secondary role."[11] The average American adult reads fewer than nine books annually, and spends seventeen times as much time watching television as reading (including all reading—magazines, newspapers, etc.). In 2004, the National Endowment for the Arts (NEA) published a study that noted a significant decline in the reading of literature in America, documenting not only lack of literacy

11. Daniel J. Boorstin, *The Image: A Guide to Pseudo-Events in America* (New York: Atheneum, 1975), 13.

per se, but especially lack of literacy in literature. In two decades alone, from 1982 to 2002, there was a 10 percent decline in literary reading among adults in the United States.[12] Dana Gioia, the chairman of the NEA, said this: "Advanced literacy is a specific intellectual skill and social habit that depends on a great many educational, cultural, and economic factors. As more Americans lose this capability, our nation becomes less informed, active, and independent-minded. These are not qualities that a free, innovative, or productive society can afford to lose."[13] As a consequence of this cultural shift, those human sensibilities (one's capacities to know, understand, experience, or appreciate certain realities) essential to expository preaching have largely disappeared, so that a theological seminary attempting to teach a person who is not comfortable with texts or with writing organized prose is analogous to a theological seminary attempting to teach a dachshund to speak French.

We will explore this idea in just a little more detail below, but let me introduce the matter here. Education through the mid-twentieth century was largely textual. People not only read, but they read literary products wherein *how* something was said was as important as *what* was said. Some call this process "reading texts," because other kinds of reading do not engage this faculty of appreciating *how* something is said. When one "reads" a phone book, scanning for information, one is not doing the same thing as when one reads a Shakespearean sonnet.

---

12. *Reading at Risk: A Survey of Literary Reading in America*, Research Division Report No. 46 (Washington, DC: National Endowment for the Arts, 2004), 21.

13. Ibid., vii.

When one "reads" the Kinsey report on human sexuality, one is not doing the same thing as when one reads Leo Tolstoy's *Anna Karenina*, although human sexuality is certainly addressed in each work. And when one reads most books about history, one is not doing the same thing as when one reads John Milton's *Paradise Lost*. While our culture has not yet become entirely illiterate, it has become almost illiterate regarding the close reading of *texts*.[14]

Further, our culture has become increasingly *aliterate*. I was first introduced to the term *aliterate* in a private conversation with Dr. James Billington, current Librarian of Congress, who spoke about studies on the phenomenon of people who *can* read but do *not* read (the concern of the previously mentioned NEA report). As the reader might expect, longitudinal studies indicate that aliteracy is advancing at a slow, steady, albeit disconcerting, rate. And more importantly for our purposes, our culture has become illiterate of texts. People do not read texts—books in which *how* the thing is said is as important as *what* is said. Similarly, people who can "reach out and touch" with a telephone or cell phone do not compose. They do occasionally write grocery lists or notes, but they do not compose. They do not sit down with scratch paper or a legal pad to sketch out an outline, and then modify that outline several times before beginning to write. Their telephone conversations show nothing of the art of personal correspondence that characterized the typical Civil War soldier writing home, for instance.

14. Cf. Allan Bloom's stimulating "The Study of Texts," in *Giants and Dwarves: Essays 1960–1990* (New York: Touchstone, 1990), 295–314.

Our culture's sensibility of composed, thoughtfully organized communication has disappeared as a common trait, and is now practiced mainly by authors.[15] In a little more detail below, I will attempt to demonstrate that these cultural changes, and especially changes in the dominant media, have created a Johnny who can neither read nor write *as he could in the early twentieth century*, and who, *therefore*, cannot preach.

My basic assumption in what follows is the primary assumption of all who study media ecology: that the various human sensibilities are shaped by social environment. A child who grows up in France speaks French, whereas one who grows up in the United States speaks (something like) English. Not only does one speak French and the other English, each learns more than the bare minimum necessary to survive; each learns the rhythms and cadences of his language, the distinctive sounds of his own language that permit him to take pleasure in its articulate or artful use. Neither child *chooses* his language; his culture chooses it for him. Only years later, if he chooses, does he augment his native language by the study of other languages. Some years before I began formal study of media ecology, I had already learned this basic reality on an intuitive level. I still recall my first experiences, well over a decade ago, at playing what I now call "The Airport Game." While wait-

---

15. I join other college professors in expressing dismay over the quality of our students' writing. It is not merely that their grammar is atrocious, spelling poor, or organization incomprehensible. Worse, they display contempt for written English. I've had students write "internet" and "Internet" interchangeably throughout a paper; such students not only have not bothered to verify the correct capitalization, but don't even make an effort to misspell consistently. E-mailers, text messagers, and IMers have been trained to regard careful writing with dismissive contempt.

ing in an airport for a flight (or while on the flight itself), one often finds oneself chatting with a total stranger. While doing this, I discovered that I could, in less than ten minutes, guess whether the stranger was a reader or not. After ten minutes or so of conversation, if I guessed that the person was a reader, I would say: "What have you been reading recently?" The stranger was ordinarily surprised, and would reply: "Well, how do you know that I read? I haven't mentioned reading anything." My answer was always the same: "Your use of language reveals it. Your language patterns are those of an individual whose use of English has been shaped by more than our generation's use of it. It is free of colloquialism and speech fads, and has obviously been developed by exposure to those who use the language well and purposefully."

The Airport Game doesn't stop here, however. I have learned that if I have twenty or thirty minutes, I can tell whether the individual writes or not; and if I have forty-five minutes to an hour, I can ordinarily successfully deduce whether the individual has studied a classical language. Those who write compose their thoughts more successfully than those who do not; they commit fewer of what I inelegantly call "sentence farts," in which one begins a sentence, partway through realizes that it cannot be successfully completed, and therefore begins again. I've known some individuals who take three or four efforts to get through fairly straightforward sentences; such individuals are never writers. They don't write editorials, or letters, or journal entries, or anything else that requires time and thought. But writers become accustomed to composing their thoughts when they write, and this compositional sensibility spills over into their spoken use of the language. They successfully employ lengthier sentences, sentences with several subordinate clauses; and they do so with nary a sentence fart. Discovering those who have studied a classical language such as Latin or Greek is a little more difficult, and takes a little more time, but it can be done also. The highly inflected nature of classical languages creates an attentiveness to grammatical detail that causes an individual to be very precise. Specific words are ordinarily preferred to general words, for instance. Further, the inflections of Greek and Latin nouns tend to create an awareness of English case usage, even though English tends now to inflect only some pronouns. Those who consistently know when to say "she and I," as opposed to "her and me," are almost always those who have studied a classical language (and one of my special joys in life occurs when those who routinely misuse English case "correct" me for using it correctly). The Airport Game has never been scientifically tested, but I also don't recall ever being wrong.

The Airport Game proves correct the basic premise of the media ecologists: that our various human sensibilities are shaped (or remain dormant) by the social environment that nurtures us. Most media ecologists are not determinists; they recognize that individuals who are perceptive enough to know their own cultures can choose to undertake efforts to shape themselves in ways that their culture does not. But apart from such activity, one's sensibilities (one's capacities to know, understand, experience, or appreciate certain realities) are determined by one's culture. What follows is an abbreviated attempt to explore some of the cultural shifts of the last half of the twentieth century, especially shifts in media, in order to suggest that these shifts have led to the underdevelopment of those sensibilities that are critical to preaching well.

2

WHY JOHNNY CAN'T PREACH, PART 1: JOHNNY CAN'T READ (TEXTS)

THERE IS A PROFOUND DIFFERENCE between reading information and reading texts. The former permits a disinterest in the question of *how* the matter is composed; its interest is only in the content. Indeed, the skill of rapid reading was designed precisely to achieve better efficiency when reading for information, by actually training the mind to ignore most of the articles, prepositions, adjectives, and adverbs. But reading a text is a laboriously slow process; when one reads a text, one is reading a piece of literature that survives beyond its initial generation largely because of its manner, irrespective of its matter. What Shakespeare says about friendship between males in the first forty or so of his sonnets is not especially significant or interesting (though it is of some interest that he could write so many sonnets about male-to-male love that is not homoerotic), but *how* he talks about friendship is so profoundly artful that one is often stunned by the achievement. Yet how many people (including ministers) in our culture today are capable of reading Shakespeare's sonnets with appreciation and pleasure? How many even read a more contemporary poet such as Robert Frost, who as recently as 1961 spoke at President Kennedy's inauguration? Do poets speak at presidential inaugurations today?

When people do read today (and they don't read often), they read almost exclusively for information or content; they almost never read for the pleasure obtained by reading an author whose command of language is exceptional. Many ministers, for instance, will read the occasional book about history. But with few exceptions, the interest in historical writing resides in the *events* narrated, not in the skillfulness of the narration. I, for instance, have read most of the late Stephen Ambrose's books, and have enjoyed them. But his books are not skillfully written in a literary sense, and the pleasure I have derived from them has not been due to great literary craftsmanship. In fact, in one of his last books (on the transcontinental railroad), I noticed that one of his paragraphs occurred twice in the book, having been accidentally cut and pasted into the narrative, word for word, in two different places, about forty pages apart. This is not great craftsmanship, and not the kind of thing that happens in Shakespeare's sonnets. Ambrose had, in my judgment, two great virtues as a writer, two things that brought great pleasure to many of us. First, he loved the United States, and therefore took great interest in her more important moments. Second, he loved the way in which humans, despite their frailties and imperfections, could achieve remarkable things when remarkable circumstances required it. And because Ambrose had these two great virtues as an author, his books are very pleasant to read for any of us who either love the American experiment or love to see the image of God on display in humans (or both).

Now, some historians border on the literary. My family lives just north of Pittsburgh, and the city's own David McCullough is a historian who has developed a fairly compelling narrative style over the years. While his first book (on the Johnstown flood) doesn't demonstrate it, his later books (especially his book on John Adams, but also his volumes on the Panama Canal and the Brooklyn Bridge) disclose a command of narrative that certainly approaches artful. And the historian Perry Ellis, in his *Founding Brothers*, produced a work that could possibly survive on its literary merits alone. Many paragraphs in that book entice the reader to reread them several times, for the sheer pleasure of their artistry. Other historians could be added to such a list: James Robertson and Barbara Tuchman have developed narrative styles that are genuinely delightful; and in American religious history, George Marsden's book on Jonathan Edwards is profoundly artful. But these exceptions do not disprove the rule: that most people who read history do so because of their interest in the events narrated. While the skillfulness of the better authors may enhance the pleasure of reading their books, it does so at the implicit rather than the explicit level, and the reader doesn't ordinarily take much notice of the literary skill.

The same could be said about other genres. Ministers will also read Tom Clancy stuff, and they routinely read the latest best-selling self-help book, but as a group they are no more interested in texts than is the culture of which they are a part. They read for information or for amusement, but they do not read because they cherish the aesthetic pleasure taken in something that is well written. They notice only the content of what they read, but do not notice the subtler semi-miracle of language well employed.

How does this phenomenon affect them as preachers? Well, they read the Bible the same way they read everything else: virtually speed-reading, scanning it for its most overt *content*. *What is this passage about?* they ask as they read, but they don't raise questions about how the passage is *constructed*. It's almost as though a version of Microsoft Word were built into their brains that causes them to see some of the words in a biblical paragraph in boldface, as the theologically, spiritually, or morally important words stand out in bold from the rest of the paragraph. They read John 3:16 the same way they read Romans 5:8; each is "about" the love of God, but they don't notice much more than that, and their sermon on God's love from John 3:16 is probably not different from their sermon on God's love from Romans 5:8.[1] Thus, they never really notice (and therefore do not and cannot preach) the distinctive thing affirmed about God's love in John 3 or Romans 5.[2] All of

1. This way of illustrating the matter, if memory serves me, was suggested to me by my former colleague at Gordon-Conwell (and now dean at Calvin) Gary J. Bekker.

2. Former colleague Haddon Robinson teaches Gordon-Conwell students that a passage has both a *subject* and a *predicate*. In the example of John 3 and

their sermons are about Christian truth or theology in *general*, and the *particular* text they read ahead of time merely prompts their memory or calls their attention to one of Christianity's important realities (insofar as they perceive it). Their reading does not stimulate them to rethink anything, and since the text doesn't stimulate them particularly (but serves merely as a reminder of what they already know), their sermon is not particularly stimulating to their hearers.

Further, since they read only for the overt content, they often actually misunderstand the text, thinking it is "about" something that it really isn't about. Many of you are aware of the book *A Shepherd Looks at Psalm 23*;[3] and if not, you've heard sermons suggesting that the Twenty-third Psalm is in some way "about" God's being a shepherd. This view is actually fairly wrongheaded. *Shepherd* is obviously a figure of speech, and as with other such figures, we should attempt to understand it as its own culture did. In the ancient Near Eastern culture, monarchs were commonly referred to by this image of a shepherd, and ancient Israel was no exception. But the Twenty-third Psalm is not an agricultural psalm; it is a royal psalm, and it begins with a profound irony: King David, Israel's "shepherd," acknowledges that Yahweh is *his* shepherd, his king. The psalm goes on to demonstrate that just as Israel's royal shepherd celebrates and rests in God's royal reign, so Israel should trust the royal Yahweh

---

Romans 5, the *subject* of each is God's love, but each *predicates* a different thing about that love.

3. Phillip Keller, *A Shepherd Looks at Psalm 23* (Grand Rapids: Zondervan, 1997).

also. Anyone with literary sensibility, reading the psalm as a whole in its literary and historical context, sees this; but most ministers don't, because their literary sensibilities are undeveloped. Or, as another example, they will puzzle over the parable of the laborers in the vineyard, concerned about its apparent blunders in labor relations, without noticing that the text is perhaps "about" something that is never overtly stated: either God's free grace or, even more acutely, his grace in including in his redemptive work Gentiles in addition to Jews.

Reading texts demands a very close and intentional reading. One cannot omit a single line of a given Shakespearean sonnet; each of the fourteen lines plays a crucial role. Those who are accustomed to reading such texts read each line for *what* it contributes to the whole and *how* it does so. But those not accustomed to reading texts closely just look for what they judge to be the important words, and the concepts to which they ostensibly point, and then they give a lecture on that concept—ordinarily without making any effort to explain the passage as a whole, to demonstrate how each clause contributes to some basic overall unity. A handful of good expository preachers do not read literature, but these exceptions are almost always people who have studied a good deal more than the ordinary amount of Greek or Hebrew, and they became close readers of texts through *this* discipline, rather than through the discipline of reading verse or literature. Ancient, inflected languages require remarkable attentiveness to the smallest details; and thorough study of such languages cultivates a close reading of texts just as the study of verse does.[4]

Culturally, then, we are no longer careful, close readers of texts, sacred or secular.[5] We scan for information, but we do not appreciate literary craftsmanship. Exposition is therefore virtually a lost art. We don't really read texts to enter the world of the author and perceive reality through his vantage point; we read texts to see how they confirm what we already believe about reality. Texts are mirrors that reflect *our*selves; they are not pictures that are appreciated in *them*selves.[6] This explains, in part, the phenomenon that many Christians will read their Bibles daily for fifty years, and not have one opinion that changes in the entire fifty-year span. Texts do not change or alter or skew their perspective; texts do not move them or shape them; they merely *use* them as mnemonic devices to recall what they already

4. As recently as the mid-1980s a personal experience confirmed to me the rapidity and profundity of our cultural shift. My wife and I were invited to a dinner, and one of the other guests was a recently retired organist of one of Richmond, Virginia's prominent Episcopal churches. When the organist discovered that I was teaching Greek at Union Seminary that summer, he exclaimed, "Why, I majored in Greek at Hobart." And when I then asked him *why* he had selected Greek as his major, he replied: "Well, when I graduated from Hobart in 1928, one had only two choices for a major, Latin and Greek; and I had always despised Latin." I hardly consider this a ringing endorsement for the study of classical languages, but it struck me as profound that as recently as the first third of the twentieth century, our country had liberal-arts colleges whose *only* option for a major was one of two classical languages. By the close of the century, one would have been fortunate to find a liberal-arts college at which both are even *offered*.

5. Neil Postman justly referred to the typographic era as "the age of exposition" because the printed word cultivated the sensibility of exposition. Now we live in the age of electronic distraction, wherein we cultivate the sensibility (if it can be called that) of distracted multitasking.

6. Richard L. Pratt Jr., "Pictures, Windows, and Mirrors in Old Testament Exegesis," *Westminster Theological Journal* 45 (1983): 156–67. I am indebted to Pratt for the distinction between reading texts as pictures, mirrors, or windows.

know. They have no capacity to expound a text, or to describe what another has said and how he has said it; and they retain only the capacity to notice when something in the language of another appears to concur with their own opinions. To employ C. S. Lewis's way of stating the matter, they "use" texts but do not "receive" them.[7]

Our inability to read texts is a direct result of the presence of electronic media. The sheer pace of an electronic media–dominated culture is entirely too fast. Electronic media flash sounds and images at us at a remarkable rate of speed; and each image or sound leaves some impact on us, but greater than the impact of any individual image or sound is the entire *pace* of the life it creates. We become acclimated to distraction, to multitasking, to giving part of our attention to many things at once, while almost never devoting the entire attention of the entire soul to anything. The close reading of texts would be an antidote to such a pace because such reading is time-consuming and requires the concentration of the entire person. When reading poetry, for instance, the rhythms and cadences, the music of the language, cannot be experienced at all by scanning. One must

7. Cf. Lewis's delightful discussion of this subject in the first several chapters of his regrettably little-known *An Experiment in Criticism* (Cambridge: Cambridge University Press, 1961). Speaking of the difference between those who "receive" literature versus those who merely "use" it, he said, "The first reading of some literary work is often, to the literary, so momentous that only experiences of love, religion, or bereavement can furnish a standard of comparison. Their whole consciousness is changed. They have become what they were not before. But there is no sign of anything like this among the other sort of readers. When they have finished the story or the novel, nothing much, or nothing at all, seems to have happened to them" (ibid., 3).

read at the pace of the tongue and the ear, not at the pace of the mind's ability to grasp information. Sven Birkerts captured this reality almost perfectly:

> To read poetry as it is meant to be read, you must push your way through the shallow-field perceptual mode that modern life makes habitual. The operation is not nearly as simple as it sounds. The eye has been taught to speed across word clusters. The sound in the ear, which lags behind the eye, is usually a noise, like the garbling that comes when tape gets dragged across magnetic heads. That garble has to be slowed. First to normal speech tempo, then by half again. Otherwise the intricacy that the poet "listened" into his lines will remain unavailable.
>
> The harder it is for you to slow down, the more you need to be rescued from the twentieth century; the more you *need* poetry.[8]

Reading texts (and especially verse) cultivates the sensibility of *significance*. Verse is comparatively dense; line for line, more is in it than in prose, and much of what is there is an eye for what is significant about life. The poet stops and stares at that which most of us merely glance at; he pauses to notice what is humane, significant, and important. The poet joins King David in observing that the human is "fearfully and wonderfully made" (Ps. 139:14), and he notices, regardless of his theological beliefs, the tragicomic nature of reality surrounded by both God's

8. Sven Birkerts, *The Electric Life: Essays on Modern Poetry* (New York: William Morrow and Company, 1989), 92 (emphasis his).

judgment and his grace. Whatever else it may be, poetry is not trivial. It may be perverse or twisted, angry or bitter, rebellious or self-centered, heterodox or even blasphemous, but it is not trivial. I am inclined to agree with William Hazlitt, who argued that "all that is worth remembering of life is the poetry of it. Fear is poetry, hope is poetry, love is poetry, hatred is poetry; contempt, jealousy, remorse, admiration, wonder, pity, despair, or madness, are all poetry."[9] Reading verse rescues us from the mundaneness of life; it permits us to observe again with wonder, and shocks us out of our cynicism and joylessness. After a day in which we have been constantly distracted by electronic devices grasping for our attention, or numbed by a "to-do" list that makes even our PDA sigh with despair, we read Robert Frost's "Birches," and we are alive again—alive as humans, alert to beauty, to creation, to play.

Mundaneness is, I believe, part of the curse of Genesis 3. The earth no longer yields its bounty without toilsome labor and much frustration. Our routines make us more efficient, as we attempt to scratch out some form of survival in this cursed environment, but those same routines can make us more like cogs in a machine and less like humans. Life becomes a series of tasks, with few uninterrupted moments to pause, to reflect, to appreciate. Verse is a common-grace gift that enables us, through the fog of images and sounds, to again see ourselves and others as bearers of the image of God. When the poet stares at that which the rest of us merely glance at, he invites us to take a

9. William Hazlitt, *Critical Essays of the Nineteenth Century* (New York: Charles Scribner's Sons, 1921), 224.

longer look along with him. It is precisely this longer look that is necessary to cultivate a sensibility for the significant.

Here, the shift of dominant cultural media has been profound, because television, in contrast to poetry, is essentially trivial. Everything about it is trivial, and it is the perfect medium *for* the trivial. Because its pictures must move (and indeed, even camera angles must move, on average less than every three seconds), it captures best those things that are kinetic, that have motion. Yet few of the more significant aspects of life involve much motion: love, humility, faith, repentance, prayer, friendship, worship, affection, fear, hope, self-control. Most of what is significant about life takes place between the ears, as we make sense of life, of our place in it, and of our failures and successes, our joys, our sorrows, our fears, our loves. This world of the mind and soul is essentially a linguistic world, a nonkinetic world; a different world from the world of rapidly changing moving images.

Television (and even film) doesn't depict these realities very well, and is at its best with the superficial and trivial, which is why the late Neil Postman (in his *Amusing Ourselves to Death*) expressed a preference for *The Three Stooges* over *The MacNeil-Lehrer Report* (two stooges?). Neither program was significant, but one had the *pretense* of significance, and it was this pretense that irked Postman. Only by televised news' own silly standards could someone spend ten to fifteen minutes on a matter of public interest and consider this to be "in-depth" coverage. Nothing of public importance can be covered in ten minutes; few important matters can even be adequately *introduced* in ten minutes. A culture that reads can consider what is significant because reading takes time, and that which is significant ordinarily takes time to apprehend. But a culture that is accustomed to commercial interruptions every six or seven minutes loses its ability to discuss significant matters because it has lost the patience necessary to consider them.

To illustrate this principle, since I was in college during the latter part of the Vietnam War (and carried a draft card for a while, and was relieved when Richard Nixon ended the draft), I decided a couple of years ago to attempt to begin to understand the Vietnam conflict and its effects on our nation. So I decided, as an introduction, to read about five books. I wanted to read the indictment of McNamara et al. in H. R. McMaster's *Dereliction of Duty*; I certainly wanted to read McNamara's own *In Retrospect*; a colleague in our history department recommends George Herring's *America's Longest War*, so I wanted to read it, and a couple other books on the topic. So I read those five books and believe that I got a general, basic orientation on a matter in our history that few of us could understand very clearly while we were going through it. Anyone who reads normally assumes that you need to read a minimum of three to five books just to get a general introduction to a subject. But the time I spent in my little five-book introduction to this matter would have translated to the longest television documentary Ken Burns has ever done! As a medium, reading cultivates a patient, lengthy attention span, whereas television as a medium is *im*patient. One is therefore suited to what is significant; the other merely to what is insignificant.

As our culture has become a television culture, therefore, a larger part of our waking life has been occupied by considering what is insignificant and unimportant (or, worse, by inadequately considering what is significant through an insignificant medium). This is part of the thesis of David Denby's wonderful volume *Great Books*.[10] Denby recounts how he returned, in middle age, to Columbia (where he had attended college) to take again the required Western civilization curriculum. The book is a delightful discussion of students, teachers, and some of the books themselves, but especially of Denby's own growing discovery that his culture and profession (film critic, along with Anthony Lane, for the *New Yorker*) had dragged him into the irony and cynicism that results from constantly giving one's attention to the insignificant. Denby observed the following about his son:

> Max was not merely a TV-watcher, as I was when I was his age in the early fifties. He was engulfed by the media—by television and to a lesser extent radio, but also by movies, video- and audiotapes, comics, activity books, computer games, Nintendo systems and the portable Game Boy as well as all the electronic games he occasionally visited in arcades.
>
> So, individually, none of these things struck me then or now as harmful. But collectively, I'm not so sure. Even if the child's character is not formed by a single TV show,

10. David Denby, *Great Books* (New York: Touchstone, 1996).

movie, video or computer game, the endless electronic assault obviously leaves its marks all over him. . . . The child survives, but along the way he becomes a kind of cynic; or rather he becomes an ironist, a knowing ironist of waste. He knows that everything in the media is transient, *disposable*. Everything on television is just for the moment—it's just *television*—and the kids pick up this derisive tone, the sense that nothing is truly serious. As they get older, David Letterman functions as their prince of irony: They learn from him that every part of their identity can be taken back; everything is a role, a put-on.[11]

Denby recognized that our electronic media–dominated culture has robbed us of the reflection about life and its meaning that had previously been fairly common:

The courses in the Western classics force us to ask all those questions about self and society we no longer address without embarrassment—the questions our media-trained habits of irony have tricked us out of asking. In order to ask those questions, students need to be enchanted before they are disenchanted. They need to love the text before they attack the sub-text. They need to read before they disappear into the aridities of electronic "information."[12]

As Denby observed the "culture wars" taking place in the universities in the late 1990s regarding the so-called

11. Ibid., 71–72.
12. Ibid., 463.

Western canon, he determined that both left and right were almost entirely wrong:

> By the end of my year in school, I knew that the culture-ideologues, both left and right, are largely talking nonsense. Both groups simplify and caricature the Western tradition. They ignore its ornery and difficult books; they ignore its actual students, most of whom have been dispossessed. Whether white, black, Asian, or Latino, American students rarely arrive at college as habitual readers, which means that few of them have more than a nominal connection to the past. It is absurd to speak, as does the academic left, of classic Western texts dominating and silencing everyone but a ruling elite of white males. The vast majority of white students do not know the intellectual tradition that is allegedly theirs any better than black or brown ones do. They have not read its books, and when they do read them, they may respond well, but they will not respond in the way that the academic left supposes. For there is only one "hegemonic discourse" in the lives of American undergraduates, and that is the mass media. Most high schools can't begin to compete against a torrent of imagery and sound that makes every moment but the present seem quaint, bloodless, or dead.[13]

We cannot pretend that we are not part of this culture, and we cannot safely continue to ignore the observations of early critics such as Jacques Ellul (especially his *The Humiliation of the Word*) and Marshall McLuhan, or more recent

13. Ibid., 459.

ones such as Postman, Denby, Sven Birkerts (*The Gutenberg Elegies*), and Todd Gitlin, who also observed the triviality of our dominating electronic media:

> To put this another way: alongside specific effects, much of the time the everyday noise of media is the buzz of the inconsequential, the *just there*. This is neither the media's downside nor their saving grace. The buzz of the inconsequential is the media's essence. This pointlessness is precisely what we are, by and large, not free *not* to choose.[14]

We are swamped by the inconsequential, bombarded by images and sounds that rob us of the opportunity for reflection and contemplation that are necessary to reacquaint ourselves with what is significant: "According to a widely cited 1989 study by Kiku Adatto, the average weekday network news sound bite from a presidential candidate shrank from 42.3 seconds in 1968 to 9.8 seconds in 1988 (with only 1 percent of the bites lasting as long as 40 seconds that year). By 2000, the average was 7.8 seconds."[15]

What kinds of ministers does such a culture produce? Ministers who are not at home with what is significant; min-

---

14. Todd Gitlin, *Media Unlimited: How the Torrent of Images and Sounds Overwhelms Our Lives* (New York: Henry Holt, 2002), 9 (emphases his). Cf. also Jacques Ellul, *The Technological Society*, trans. John Wilkinson (New York: Knopf, 1964); Jacques Ellul, *The Humiliation of the Word*, trans. Joyce Main Hanks (Grand Rapids: Eerdmans, 1985); Marshall McLuhan, *Understanding Media: The Extensions of Man* (New York: McGraw-Hill, 1964); Neil Postman, *Amusing Ourselves to Death: Public Discourse in the Age of Television* (New York: Viking, 1985); Neil Postman, *Technopoly: The Surrender of Culture to Technology* (New York: Vintage Books, 1993); Sven Birkerts, *The Gutenberg Elegies: The Fate of Reading in an Electronic Age* (New York: Ballantine Books, 1995).

15. Gitlin, *Media Unlimited*, 96.

isters whose attention span is less than that of a four-year-old in the 1940s, who race around like the rest of us, constantly distracted by sounds and images of inconsequential trivialities, and out of touch with what is weighty. It is not surprising that their sermons, and the alleged worship that surrounds them, are often trifling, thoughtless, uninspiring, and mundane. It is not surprising that their sermons are mindlessly practical, in the "how-to" sense. It is also not surprising that their sermons tend to be moralistic, sentimentalistic, or slavishly drafted into the so-called culture wars. The great seriousness of the reality of being human, the dreadful seriousness of the coming judgment of God, the sheer insignificance of the present in light of eternity—realities that once were the subtext of virtually every sermon—have now disappeared, and have been replaced by one triviality after another.[16]

In a sense, then, the few conversations there have been about preaching and preachers in the last generation have been relatively pointless. Whether a sermon is preached by a man or a woman is comparatively unimportant; whether it encourages a liberal or conservative sociopolitical agenda is

16. While it is not my purpose here to present an in-depth discussion of the so-called contemporary worship that has crept across the Christian landscape like a plague, I must observe here how profoundly trite it ordinarily is. Pop music, as an idiom, simply cannot address that which is weighty (though folk music can, classical music can, and sometimes blues or jazz can); its idiom itself is faddish, glib, superficial. Therefore, serious lyrics don't fit in this idiom (nor does there appear to be any effort to accomplish this). Though lamentable, it is not at all surprising to me that the church in a trivial culture becomes a trivial church with trivial liturgy. I am fairly seriously considering following this book with another: *Why Johnny Can't Sing Hymns.*

comparatively inconsequential; whether its "how-to" advice or pop psychology is helpful or not makes little difference. What would make a difference would be Christian proclamation that is consequential, that is concerned less with current events than with the history-encompassing events of creation, fall, and redemption. What would make a difference would be Christian proclamation that did not panic every time a court rendered a decision on some pet geopolitical concern, but called our attention instead to the certain judgment of God, with whom we have to do. What would make a difference would be Christian proclamation that was less concerned with "how-to" and more concerned with "why-to," why humans are fearfully and wonderfully made in the image of God. What might make a difference would be Christian proclamation that was less concerned with the latest news from the Beltway, and more concerned with the stunning and perennial good news that God in Christ is reconciling sinners to himself. But any one of these preferred alternatives requires a sensibility for the significant; a capacity to distinguish the weighty from the light, and the consequential from the trivial.

3

WHY JOHNNY CAN'T PREACH, PART 2: JOHNNY CAN'T WRITE

EVERY TECHNOLOGICAL DEVELOPMENT has a cost that is well beyond what is expended in research and development. Every technological development has an opportunity cost because once we spend even part of our day using a technology we once did *not* use, some of the things we once did with our time we no longer do. This is especially true, and especially significant, when the technology is in the area of media. When oral cultures become writing cultures, they change profoundly.[1] When writing cultures develop the printing press, so that books (unlike manuscripts) become affordable and available, things change even more. Believers today have great difficulty even imagining

1. Walter Ong, *Orality and Literacy: The Technologizing of the Word* (New York: Routledge, 1982); Eric A. Havelock, *The Muse Learns to Write: Reflections on Orality and Literacy from Antiquity to the Present* (New Haven, CT: Yale University Press, 1986).

what it was like to be a believer in the first fifteen centuries of the church, when no individual owned books (and therefore no individual owned a Bible); when the entire encounter with inscripturated revelation was exclusively in the public reading of the Bible in the liturgy.[2] Our very approach to religion and piety itself is shaped by a technological development, the printing press. Some of our day is expended in reading, which far less than 1 percent of Christians would have ever done before the fifteenth century.

Beginning in the late nineteenth century, our culture witnessed a cluster of new communication technologies every bit as significant as writing or the printing press—the various electronic media that began with Samuel Morse's telegraph and have developed into cell phones, e-mail, and instant messaging, and the image-based medium of photography. The telephone has radically and profoundly altered the shape of society and of individual consciousness. All electronic media break the barrier of space; we can speak to people to whom we are not physically proximate. The telephone permits us to speak to a person on the other end of our street, or on the other end of the world. This technology has its advantages:

2. We sometimes overlook the extraordinary when it occurs in the New Testament because we project our own typographic era back into the biblical era. We read of the Ethiopian in Acts 8, ordinarily without any wonder over the remarkable reality that the Ethiopian had a text of Isaiah with him. We just think of him as a commuter, reading his Bible on the way to work. In fact, in the ancient world handwritten manuscripts were extremely rare, and extremely expensive, and this Ethiopian would not even have had *access* to a scroll of Isaiah were it not for the fact that, professionally, he was the keeper of the treasure of Queen Candace (Acts 8:27). He was like a museum curator today—an individual who had access to virtually priceless artifacts.

when someone suddenly becomes ill, we can call for an ambulance to be dispatched to the scene with lifesaving speed. But disadvantages attend these technological developments also, and while we cannot discuss all of them here, we must consider two: that we can hear people whom we do not see, and that we do not compose our thoughts as frequently or carefully as we once did.

We are all glad that we can speak to people whom we cannot see (and who cannot see us). I can be running around in the morning in my boxer shorts with a toothbrush in my hand, opening the door for a family cat to run outside, while carrying on a conversation with someone who probably wouldn't care to see me in that condition (indeed, I myself avoid interactions with mirrors under such circumstances). But this lack of visible response in conversation makes us literalists, whose capacity to see and interpret body language, gestures, and the language of the eyes atrophies because of comparatively infrequent use. When conversing with a person who is visibly present, for instance, we can "read" their reaction to a change in conversation topic, and determine that the other individual is apparently not interested in the topic. We can notice when people appear uncomfortable with a given topic, or when they avert our gaze. But when "conversing" on the telephone, all we have is the voice; and while tone can tell us something (in addition to the actual words themselves), tone can rarely tell us as much as does the enormous range of body-language clues. Silence also seems more awkward on the telephone because nothing is visibly happening to complement the words. By contrast, when sitting on a front porch together and chatting with someone else, that person can nod agreeingly to something we say without saying anything, and we understand that the person is perhaps pondering the point further, or pleased to hear that we agree.

Now, the obvious point of this for preaching is this: If we become less practiced (and therefore less skilled) at reading people's visible reactions to our speech, we will become less skilled at reading those reactions when speaking publicly. In the monologue of a sermon, for instance, the hearers do not speak at all, but they do reply visibly, if we are alert to notice. We can notice whether people appear to be following with interest or whether they appear to be entirely uninterested, and we can adjust our volume, our tone, our manner, or our vocabulary to be sure that they have followed the current point before we move to another. Indeed, I have sometimes preached in buildings that were sufficiently hot to flush the faces of one or two people. As I noticed this, I quickly thought about which points of the sermon could be omitted without substantial loss, omitted them, and finished the sermon earlier than usual, because the visual feedback assured me that the congregation's attention would necessarily wane because of the heat. But ministers today seem especially blind to the visible response of the congregation because, as a culture, we get used to telephone conversations in which there *is* no visible response. On occasion when suffering through an unusually bad sermon, I have glanced around to observe others in the congregation, and noticed that virtually no one in the congregation was looking at the minister. He had lost the entire congregation, yet seemed oblivious to the fact that he had done so.

As a medium, the telephone also robs us of composition skills. When writing a letter, one takes as much time as necessary to think about what one wishes to say, and why, and how. One can even write out an outline on a piece of scratch paper, or even an entire first draft. But on the telephone, even when we have called for a particular purpose, sometimes the person on the other end of the line says something off the topic, and courtesy requires that we make some polite response, and since neither party relishes silence in that medium, before long twenty minutes have passed in mindless, insignificant babble, and we haven't yet said what we intended to say when we called. While we certainly take an instinctive and appropriate pleasure in the very sound of the voice of someone we love, a great deal is also lost when we become accustomed to noncomposed thought and speech, and unaccustomed to composed thought and speech.

When I was in college, my habit was to write to my parents weekly. Ordinarily, at least one (sometimes both) replied weekly as well. In those letters, I had opportunity to distinguish the significant from the insignificant, and to limit myself to a few pages at the most. If I still had those letters, and if I did a word count on them, they would undoubtedly prove to be one-fourth to one-fifth the size (if not smaller) of the transcript of a typical telephone conversation. We say more *words* on the telephone, but I don't believe we say more significant *things*; to the contrary, I think the telephone carries the insignificant as comfortably as the significant. But a letter would appear absolutely foolish if it were filled with the kind of insignificance that is common in a telephone conversation. And of course, since the telephone is a form of dialogue (not monologue), composition is virtually impossible, and we lose the instinctive habit of asking: *What should I say first, this or that?*

The consequences of this for preaching should be very obvious. Telephone conversations rarely have unity, order, or movement; it isn't surprising that those who spend more time on the phone than in private written correspondence preach sermons that rarely have unity, order, or movement. While ministers make some effort in the pulpit to avoid the worst colloquialisms, and while they ordinarily have learned to slow their rate of speech, in many other respects their sermons reflect the babbling, rambling quality of a typical telephone conversation. The discourse consists of a series of unrelated observations that occurred to the minister as he read the passage (or other books about the passage), but there is little apparent unity or organization. Further, ministers display very little judgment about what is significant and what is insignificant. Virtually every sentence comes out in the same tone, and the hearers strain to attempt to discover what the minister thinks is *significant* in all of this—not always successfully. And this failure arises partly because we have become accustomed (via the telephone) to discussing what is insignificant, and doing so in an unstructured, uncomposed manner.

In the nineteenth century, many biographers wrote books titled *The Life and Letters of So-and-So*. While this was not always an eloquent way of writing history, it speaks volumes about our cultural distance; if restricted to composing a narrative of someone's life around his written correspondence today, we wouldn't be able to write biographies, because people write too few letters to constitute the substance of a book. Further, if you read those nineteenth-century letters, you cannot fail to notice how articulate, thoughtful, and well composed they commonly are. A culture that was accustomed to thoughtful, well-composed letters produced remarkably significant letters, even among fairly common people. Today, we have become a culture of telephone babblers, unskilled at the most basic questions of composition; and it is simply too much to expect that a typical member of such a culture can be quickly trained to deliver well-composed, thoughtful sermons.

Totally apart from the possibility of individual circumstances (e.g., a minister who is too lazy to work on his sermons), the culture itself is so profoundly different from the way it was around the Second World War that we simply cannot expect members of our culture to be able to produce organized, clear expositions of ancient texts. A once-common sensibility (close reading of texts) is now uncommon, and a once-common activity (composition) is now comparatively rare. A once-common daily occurrence (face-to-face communication allowing us to "read" the unstated feelings of another) has been replaced by telephone conversation in which visual feedback is absent. A once-common sensibility, the capacity to distinguish the significant from the insignificant, is becoming rare. For a minister today to preach a basic average sermon by early-twentieth-century standards would require a lifestyle that is significantly countercultural.

Our seminary curricula are largely identical to what they were around the First World War, but the entering seminarian is a profoundly different person than was the seminarian of the early twentieth century. Then, the individual was well read in poetry, and had studied nearly a decade of classical language (Latin, Greek, or both), learning by reading poetry and ancient languages to read texts carefully. He had written compositions almost weekly in many of his academic classes, and often wrote letters to friends and family. In contrast, the entering seminarian today has the faculties of a sixth- to eighth-grader sixty years ago, and the seminary curriculum cannot make this seminarian an adult by the time he graduates.

4

A FEW THOUGHTS
ABOUT CONTENT

EARLY ON, I DETERMINED that this book would be an
assessment of Christian preaching in the generic sense. To
that end, I have made a studied effort to avoid and evade the
"hot-button" issues in preaching today. At the risk of running afoul of one or two of those issues, I wish to address
the matter of the *content* of preaching, because in addition
to the cultural matters that have concerned me throughout,
I also believe that preaching today fails almost entirely in
its content. Even when one can discern a unified point in a
sermon, it is sometimes a point hardly worth making, and
certainly not worth making in a Christian pulpit during a
service of worship. So I wish to address briefly what I believe
the content of preaching should be, and what its common
alternatives are.

From about twenty-five years of wrestling with the question, I have come to concur with those who believe that

the content of Christian preaching should be the person, character, and work of Christ. What we declare, with Paul, is not ourselves, but Christ crucified. Our message, like Paul's, is "the message of the cross" (1 Cor. 1:18). The substance of our proclamation is the soteric fitness of the person and character of Christ, and the soteric competence of his work. With the old Puritan John Flavel, we wish to open up that "Fountain of Life" which consists of Christ's "Essential [person of Christ] and Mediatorial [work of Christ] Glory."[1] What is offered to the congregation, in rightly ordered Christian worship, is nothing less than Christ himself.[2]

Now, since Christ rescues us from both the guilt and the power of sin, one aspect of his work is the work of sanctification, whereby he renews us into the image of God and conforms us to his own likeness. So Christian proclamation properly includes the shaping of a Christian moral vision, and preaching Christ crucified does not exclude, but intentionally includes, such a vision. But it is never appropriate, in my estimation, for one word of moral counsel ever to proceed from a Christian pulpit that is not clearly, in its context,

1. Flavel's "Fountain of Life" consists of forty-three sermons—six on the person of Christ and thirty-seven on the work of Christ. If we were to compare contemporary preaching to this standard, we would honestly be able to call it only a "Dribble of Life."

2. And here, the difference between historic Protestantism and Roman Catholicism is almost total. In Rome's understanding of the Supper, Christ is offered *up*, to the Father; in the Protestant understanding, Christ is offered *down* (as it were), to God's elect. Protestants can easily and happily agree, therefore, that there is a true "offering" of Christ in the sacrament; but we believe he is offered again to *us*, not sacrificially to the Father, whose wrath against the elect has been appeased forever by the once-offered sacrifice of Christ on the cross.

redemptive. That is, even when the faithful exposition of particular texts requires some explanation of aspects of our behavior, it is always to be done in a manner that the hearer perceives such commended behavior to be itself a matter of being rescued from the power of sin through the grace of Christ. When properly done, the hearer longs to be rescued from that depravity from which no sinner can rescue himself; and the hearer rejoices to know that a kind and gracious God is both willing and able to begin that rescue, which will be completed in glorification.

This focus on the person and work of Christ includes the character of Christ. Ordinarily, when people discuss "the person of Christ," they refer to such matters as his human and divine natures, his sinlessness, and so on. Without excluding such matters, it is important to include the character of Christ under the person of Christ, especially insofar as his character is soterically significant. Thus, Jesus refers to himself as "meek and lowly of heart"; the author of Hebrews refers to him as "faithful" over God's house, and as a "sympathetic" High Priest. Christian proclamation properly includes a declaration of those character traits that equip Christ to effectually fulfill his redemptive office. His love, mercy, compassion, and other traits equip him in specific ways to accomplish his work; therefore, the proclamation of such traits nourishes the faith of those who come to God through him.

Many other homileticians have made this plea for what I might call "Christ-centered" preaching. Robert Lewis

Dabney, referred to in chapter I, was speaking of this when he mentioned that one of the cardinal requisites of a sermon is its "evangelical tone." Dabney was not referring merely or primarily to some stylistic trait in the delivery of the sermon; he was referring to its content as being essentially *evangelical,* in the nineteenth-century sense of the term. At that time, *evangelical* had not yet become wedded to revivalism; rather, like its German counterpart, *evangelisch,* it referred to the whole of Protestant soteriology, as expressed in the historic Protestant creeds.

> First, then, this attitude dictates that the *matter* of the sermon shall be prevalently evangelical [emphasis mine]. We cannot better describe it than in the words of the apostles, when they so frequently speak of their work as "preaching Christ," or "preaching Christ crucified." We do not conceive that they mean to declare, the only facts they ever recited were those enacted on Calvary, or that they limited themselves exclusively to the one doctrine of vicarious satisfaction for sin. . . . But we find that these facts and this doctrine were central to their teachings. They recurred perpetually with a prominence suitable to their importance. More than this, they were ever near at hand, as the *focus* to which every beam of divine truth must converge [emphasis his].[3]

Note Dabney's suggestion that in apostolic times, the realities of Calvary and substitutionary atonement "recurred

3. Robert Lewis Dabney, *Sacred Rhetoric: or a Course of Lectures on Preaching* (Edinburgh: Banner of Truth, 1979), 114.

perpetually with a prominence suitable to their importance." What could we conclude about preaching today, other than that the great transaction of the Sin-bearer's suffering for sinners has receded in importance from our churches? Many, many things feature more prominently in (allegedly) Christian proclamation today, with the necessary logical corollary that they are deemed more important than the atonement.

In our own generation, the late Ed Clowney was well known for his advocacy of Christ-centered preaching, and Bryan Chapell, from Covenant Seminary, advocates the same.[4] Indeed, Chapell teaches his students a very helpful way to do this—that they always study a given text with an eye toward its FCF (its "fallen-condition focus"): how does a given text address us in some specific aspect of our fallen condition, so that it points us to the remedy for that condition in the redemptive work of Christ?[5]

With Clowney and Chapell, I believe Christian proclamation should be Christ-centered. I believe this because I am a student of the New Testament, and I believe that the New Testament teaches this principle. Not only does Paul

4. Edmund P. Clowney, *Preaching Christ in All of Scripture* (Wheaton, IL: Crossway, 2003); Bryan Chapell, *Christ-Centered Preaching: Redeeming the Expository Sermon* (Grand Rapids: Baker, 1994). This outstanding contemporary work on homiletics begins, in the preface, with this important sentence: "The two words about which the whole of this work could be wrapped are *authority* and *redemption*" (p. 11). Chapell's instruction regarding exposition reflects his understanding of divine authority, and his instruction regarding Christ-centeredness reflects his concern that Christian proclamation be redemptive. Dennis Johnson has ably contributed to this approach in his recently published *Him We Proclaim: Preaching Christ from All of Scripture* (Phillipsburg, NJ: P&R Publishing, 2007).

5. Chapell, *Christ-Centered Preaching*, esp. 40–44.

routinely characterize his comments about preaching this way, but others do also. When Jesus talks with Peter about whether Peter loves him, he replies: "Feed my lambs. . . . Tend my sheep. . . . Feed my sheep" (John 21:15–17). Contextually, I would argue that these are not three different things, but one thing stated in three ways (note that the verb "feed" has both "lambs" and "sheep" as its direct objects, and both verbs, "feed" and "tends," have "sheep" as their object). That is, the particular "tending" referred to here is the pastoral care that ensures that the flock is *fed*. Such nourishment and spiritual sustenance, I would argue, comes from proclaiming the fitness and competence of Christ in his mediatorial work. When we "feed" God's flock, we feed their *faith*. We nourish the part of them that has the need and capacity to rest on Christ and have confidence in his work of redemption.

This was also John Calvin's view. Ordinarily, the relation of Word and sacrament is very strong for Calvin.[6] Each complements the other and aids the other in fulfilling its proper task. "For we ought to understand the word not as one whispered without meaning and without faith, a mere noise, like a magic incantation, which has the force to consecrate the element. Rather, it should, when preached, make us understand what the visible sign means."[7] But how can the preaching help us understand what baptism or the

---

6. Cf. the outstanding exposition of Calvin's thought in this area in Ronald S. Wallace, *Calvin's Doctrine of the Word and Sacrament* (Grand Rapids: Eerdmans, 1957).

7. John Calvin, *Institutes of the Christian Religion*, ed. John T. McNeill, trans. Ford Lewis Battles (Philadelphia: Westminster, 1960), 4.14.4.

Lord's Supper means, unless the preaching is essentially and profoundly Christological? As Wallace observes on the above-referenced section of Calvin's *Institutes*: "In the use of the sacraments it is of the utmost importance not only that the Word be given but that those who participate attend first to the Word and then relate the sacramental action to the Word that has been spoken, otherwise the sacraments will lose their value."[8] Calvin even believed that the entire Old Testament Scriptures were a foreshadowing of Christ. Unlike so many (culture warrior?) ministers today, who view Israel as a type or example of properly ordered societies or as an example of our own trials, Calvin viewed Israel as a type of Christ. As Wallace summarized Calvin's view: "The sufferings of the faithful in Israel are adumbrations of the sufferings of Christ."[9] And it need hardly be said that this was Martin Luther's view before Calvin. Every Lutheran sermon has two basic parts: law and gospel. In the first, God's demand on his creature is articulated; and in the second, God's provision in Christ for the failure to keep his demand is presented. Thus, every rightly ordered Lutheran sermon has always presented Christ, as the gracious Redeemer of the guilty.

Such Christological preaching feeds the soul and builds faith. Faith is not built by preaching introspectively (constantly

---

8. Wallace, *Calvin's Doctrine*, 137. And note that the passage in Calvin was not using "word" to mean the "words of institution" regarding the sacrament, but the Word "when preached." Thus Calvin, and his twentieth-century student Ronald Wallace, understood that preaching should ordinarily "make us understand what the visible sign means."

9. Ibid., 43. Cf. Wallace's entire section: "The Form of Christ as Foreshadowed in the Old Testament" (pp., 42–59).

challenging people to question whether they *have* faith); faith is not built by preaching moralistically (which has exactly the opposite effect of focusing attention on the *self* rather than on Christ, in whom our faith is placed); faith is not built by joining the culture wars and taking potshots at what is wrong with our culture. Faith is built by careful, thorough exposition of the person, character, and work of Christ.

One of the great articulations of this reality in the history of Christian literature occurs in a letter written by Clement Read Vaughan to the renowned Southern Presbyterian theologian Robert Lewis Dabney. Dabney moved from Virginia to Austin, Texas, almost twenty years after the Civil War and lived there for another fifteen years. In his latter years, he became blind and weak, and knew his death was near. He wrote to his old friend Vaughan, wondering whether he would have strong enough faith to face his impending death, and Vaughan's reply was as theologically trenchant as it was pastorally lovely. He wrote back to Dabney and asked Dabney what a traveler would do if he came to a chasm over which a bridge was spanned:

> What does he do to breed confidence in the bridge? He looks at the bridge; he gets down and examines it. He don't [sic] stand at the bridge-head and turn his thoughts curiously in on his own mind to see if he has confidence in the bridge. If his examination of the bridge gives him a certain amount of confidence, and yet he wants more, how does he make his faith grow? Why, in the same way; he still continues to examine the bridge. Now, my dear

old man, let your faith take care of itself for awhile, and you just think of what you are allowed to trust in. Think of the Master's power, think of his love; think how he is interested in the soul that searches for him, and will not be comforted until he finds him. Think of what he has done, his work. That blood of his is mightier than all the sins of all the sinners that ever lived. Don't you think it will master yours? . . .

Now, dear old friend, I have done to you just what I would want you to do to me if I were lying in your place. The great theologian, after all, is just like any other one of God's children, and the simple gospel talked to him is just as essential to his comfort as it is to a milk-maid or to a plow-boy. May God give you grace, not to lay too much stress on your faith, but to grasp the great ground of confidence, Christ, and *all his work and all his personal fitness to be a sinner's refuge.* Faith is only an eye to see him. I have been praying that God would quiet your pains as you advance, and enable you to see the gladness of the gospel at every step. Good-bye. God be with you as he will. Think of the Bridge!

Your brother,
C. R. V.[10]

I know that some today object to such an emphasis. I know that there are those who are terribly afraid that such Christ-centered preaching will lead to licentiousness; but

10. Thomas Cary Johnson, *The Life and Letters of Robert Lewis Dabney* (Edinburgh: Banner of Truth, 1977), 480 (emphasis mine).

I categorically deny it. I've witnessed with my own eyes the difference between believers who suffer through moralistic preaching and those who experience Christological preaching. The former are never as strong or vibrant in their Christian discipleship as the latter. In theory, we all say we believe, for instance, that good works are the "inevitable" fruit of saving faith. I not only say this; I believe it.

I believe that as people's confidence in Christ grows, they do, ordinarily and inevitably, bear fruit that accords with faith. Thus, there is no need for some trade-off here, or some alleged dichotomy suggesting that we need to preach morality if we are to have morality. No; preach Christ, and you will have morality. Fill the sails of your hearers' souls with the wind of confidence in the Redeemer, and they will trust him as their Sanctifier, and long to see his fruit in their lives. Fill their minds and imaginations with a vision of the loveliness and perfection of Christ in his person, and the flock will long to be like him. Impress upon their weak and wavering hearts the utter competence of the mediation of the One who ever lives to make intercession for them, and they will long to serve and comfort others, even as Christ has served and comforted them.

Some Alternatives Exposed: Four Failures

To clarify what I think Christological preaching is, it may help to contrast it with several common alternatives— alternatives that are rarely self-consciously defended or propagated despite their prevalence in practice. There are three or four of these common alternatives (depending on whether one is considered a subset of another): Moralism, How-To, Introspection, and Social Gospel/Culture War.[11]

Moralism

In the transition from the nineteenth to the twentieth century, a movement arose within Christianity called Protestant liberalism. It was a way of understanding Christianity as essentially consisting of a particular moral framework, and of understanding Christ as essentially a great moral teacher. Protestant liberalism often denied outright that Christianity was a redemptive religion; it was a religion of ethics, and what it promoted was not a set of beliefs about humans estranged from God, and how this God was reconciled through the work of his Son. Rather, it perceived Christianity as consisting of the discovery of a right and proper way to live an ethical life.[12]

Ironically, the very orthodox and evangelical Christians who protested against Protestant liberalism in the early twentieth century are quite likely to promote its basic emphases from the pulpit today. In orthodox Reformed

11. There is also the contemporaneist/emergent alternative, which is to dispense with expository preaching altogether, since it is regarded by them as passé. To many of this alternative's proponents, preaching is apparently "irrelevant." But as long as original sin has the human race in its grasp, and as long as the conscience has the slightest awareness of guilt, declaring the competence of the sin-bearing Christ to rescue the guilty will never be irrelevant.

12. The classic rebuttal to this view was J. Gresham Machen, *Christianity and Liberalism* (Grand Rapids: Eerdmans, 1923).

pulpits, one finds a frequency of moralism that would have been quite at home in the most liberal of the Protestant liberal pulpits of nearly a century ago. Laymen, and even some officers, don't notice this because they use the terms *liberal* and *conservative* as the network news anchors have taught them to use them. They think liberalism is a certain *kind* of ethics, different from conservative ethics. But in terms of church history, liberalism was an understanding of Christianity that wished to embrace its ethical system without its redemptive system, and the ethical system of the classic Protestant liberal was largely orthodox and correct. Therefore, Christian proclamation that effectively emphasizes morality rather than redemption is Protestant liberal proclamation.

Moralism occurs whenever the fundamental message of a sermon is "be good; do good" (or some specific thereof). Whenever the fundamental purpose of the sermon is to improve the behavior of others, so that Christ in his redemptive office is either denied or largely overlooked, the sermon is moralistic. Such moralism is so common in American pulpits that when in ordinary conversation one individual attempts to correct another's behavior, it is not uncommon to hear the reply: "Oh, so you're going to preach to me now, are you?" People have obviously come to associate preaching with moral improvement (or moral scolding); they do not associate preaching with a proclamation of the fitness of Christ's person and the adequacy of his work to save to the uttermost those who come to God through him.

If you read Luther's comments about his life as a monk before his conversion, you will find Luther talking about how all he ever heard from the church was "do this" and "don't do that." He did not hear that there was a Mediator, a Redeemer, who had rescued those who had done wrong from the coming judgment of God. Oh, it might have been mentioned as an aside from time to time, but the dominant theme that he heard again and again was "do this; don't do that." Then go and listen to the typical sermon in the typical evangelical or Reformed church, and ask what Luther would think if he were present. Luther would think he was still in Rome. Perhaps somewhere in the sermon is some mention of Christ; perhaps at the end is an obligatory comment, "And of course we couldn't do this apart from the grace of God in Christ"—but such a lame comment cannot rescue an essentially moralistic sermon and make it redemptive. One cannot expend thirty-eight minutes describing the difference between right and wrong, and then rescue the sermon in the final two minutes. Not only is the hearer already numb by now, overwhelmed and overcome by the recognition that his life is out of accord with God's wishes, but he has grown weary by the message, and hardly even notices when the minister pulls Christ, like a rabbit out of a magician's hat, from the black hole of the moralistic sermon at the last minute.

How-To

How-to preaching could easily be considered a subset of moralism, and I sometimes consider it to be so myself.

But a small difference of emphasis causes some to see it as a separate category, and I will present it as such here. How-to preaching differs from moralism not so much in the *what* as in the *how*. Unlike moralism, it expends less time describing *what* one ought to do, and more time *how* to go about doing it. In one sense, it is even worse than moralism, because it reduces life and religion to technique, and suggests (implicitly, never explicitly) that a sinner *can* change his ways if he just has the right method.[13] I would love to challenge the how-to preacher to preach a sermon on "How the Leopard Can Change His Spots," since, biblically, this is as easily done as a sinner's changing his ways.

How-to preaching, like moralism, pushes the person and work of the redeeming Christ out of the realm of the hearer's consideration. The hearer's utter inability to rescue himself from sin, and Christ's utter ability to do precisely that, would not be at home in such a homiletical environment. The how-to sermon implies that human behavior is not a matter of an intractable will, not a matter of total depravity, not a matter of rebellion against the reign of God the Creator, but merely a matter of technique. It is worse than Pelagianism because it doesn't even accept the burden of attempting to *prove* that the will is morally unencumbered by original sin; it *assumes* this heresy from the outset.

13. I am indebted to my former colleague at Gordon-Conwell, David F. Wells, for this insight regarding technique. I don't recall now whether Wells was influenced by Jacques Ellul, but my subsequent reading of Ellul revealed a similar concern to that which Wells had articulated. Most cultural observers see this as a by-product of modernity, with its tendency to believe that all problems can be solved through technique or technology.

Introspection

Some of the neo-Puritans have apparently determined that the purpose and essence of Christian preaching is to persuade people that they do not, in fact, believe. The subtitle of each of their sermons could accurately be: "I Know You Think You Are a Christian, but You Are Not." This brand of preaching constantly suggests that if a person does not always love attending church, always look forward to reading the Bible, or family worship, or prayer, then the person is probably not a believer. To the outsider, it appears patently curious to take an opportunity to promote faith as an opportunity to declare its nonexistence; but to the insider, this doesn't appear foolish at all, and people routinely do it.

The hearer falls into one of two categories: one category of listener assumes that the minister is talking about someone *else*, and he rejoices (as did the Pharisee over the tax collector) to hear "the other guy" getting straightened out. Another category of listener eventually capitulates and says: "Okay, I'm not a believer; have it your way. I'm just a horrible, terrible person who's going to hell." But since the sermon mentions Christ only in passing (if at all), the sermon says nothing about the adequacy of Christ as Redeemer, and therefore does nothing to nourish or build faith in him. So true unbelievers are given nothing that might make believers of them, and many true believers are persuaded that they are not believers, and the consolations of Christian faith are taken from them. Such preaching hardly achieves what Westminster's Shorter Catechism 89 says; it is not a means of "building them up in holiness *and comfort, through faith, unto salvation.*"

At one point in my pilgrimage, I suffered through two years of such preaching, as did my wife. *Suffered* is not too strong a word. It is painful to hear every passage of Scripture twisted to do what only several of them actually do (i.e., warn the complacent that not everyone who says, "Lord, Lord" will enter the kingdom of heaven). And it is absolutely debilitating to be told again and again that one does not have faith when one knows perfectly well that one *does* have faith, albeit weak and imperfect. There is simply nothing for the faithful to take away from such a sermon; you have heard nothing that profits you in any way, and those at whom the sermon is directed ordinarily do not profit because the self-righteous always assume the minister is talking about someone *else*.

So no one profits from this kind of preaching; indeed, both categories of hearer are harmed by it. But I don't expect it will end anytime soon. The self-righteous like it too much; for them, religion makes them feel good about themselves, because it allows them to view themselves as the good guys and others as the bad guys—they love to hear the minister scold the bad guys each week. And sadly, the temperament of some ministers is simply officious. Scolding others is their life calling; they have the genetic disposition to be a Jewish mother.

Social Gospel/So-Called Culture War [14]

A fourth alternative to real Christian proclamation is what would have been called the "Social Gospel" in the early twentieth century, but what is more likely to be called the "Culture Wars" today. In each case, the Christian pulpit is devoted to commenting on what's wrong with our particular culture, and what ought to be done to improve it, either by individuals or (worse) by the coercive powers of government. Since, again, the sociocultural and sociopsychological function of religion for many people is analogous to the function it had for the Pharisee (who thought himself righteous and despised others), there will always

14. I add *so-called* before *culture war* because I think the entire alleged "war" in the culture between the religious elements and the secular elements exists in the imagination. I do not deny the presence of those with a secular worldview and those with a religious worldview in our culture; I deny that there is anything new about this. Indeed, I believe much of the beauty of the work of the Founding Fathers of the American Republic was that they created a form of government that was impervious to any such wars, if citizens rightly understood what they were doing. Because individual liberty was more important for the founders than any good thing that a coercive federal government might conceivably do, the Republic was designed to be one in which religious liberty was respected and promoted, even the liberty to be irreligious. Many of the founders were essentially secularists (e.g., Thomas Jefferson), and others were ardently religious in the most orthodox sense (e.g., John Witherspoon). Jefferson never lost a night's sleep fearing that Witherspoon would use federal power to coerce him; and Witherspoon never lost a night's sleep fearing that Jefferson would use federal power to coerce him. Each believed in liberty, and was assured that the other did also. There was no "cultural war" between the two, even though there was a profound difference in worldview.

The American Republic was designed in such a manner that it could have avoided the extremes represented today by secularist France and religious Iran. France enforces secularism in public; Iran enforces religion in public. The American Republic was designed to enforce neither, but permit both. The so-called culture wars in that Republic today are therefore due to a failure to believe in liberty, and a trigger-happy willingness to coerce others.

be a warm welcome for such preaching. Many people love to live in their imagined and self-made world of good guys and bad guys, to be reminded that there are good people and bad people and that they are among the good. Indeed, the appetite for this Manichaean worldview is apparently insatiable for some; they appear psychologically incapable of functioning apart from it. And many ministers are willing to accommodate them.

What's wrong with our culture and every culture, and all human culture since Genesis 3, is that all of us (not some of us) in Adam have revolted against the reign of God, and that each of us (not some of us) prefers his own will to the will of God. Worse, we are utterly incapable, in and of ourselves, of changing. The government cannot change us or rescue us from our revolt; education cannot enlighten our darkened minds; not even the church can deliver us from our darkened understanding that considers our own way better than God's way; and surely coercive human governments cannot cure souls. Only the God-man, the last Adam, by his perfect obedience and sacrifice and present intercession at the right hand of God, can rescue any of us from our revolt. So the one inadmissible thing to a culture warrior (that cultural change is out of our hands) is the basic subtext of everything the Bible teaches.

The culture warrior refuses to acknowledge that true and significant cultural change can happen only when the individual members of the culture have forsaken their own self-centeredness, and have revolted against their revolt against

God. Worse, the culture warrior assumes that coerced change in behavior is desirable—that if we can pass a law that outlaws sin, this will somehow make people and culture better (when, in fact, we just become more devious and learn how to evade detection, adding deception to our other sins). Culture warriors are not content with the two legitimate ways in which humans may exert influence on the behavior of others: through reasoned discourse and the power of example. The power of example is too costly and too slow, and besides, we don't wish to be around unbelievers much anyway. And reasoned discourse is beyond the capacity of most of us today; most could never explain convincingly to another why one behavioral choice is wiser than another. So we resort to coercion: using the coercive power of the government to enforce external compliance to the ways of God.

Such a view is so contrary to everything the Bible teaches that its prevalence must be accounted for as a kind of blindness that is due to misplaced patriotism. All of us have blind spots, myself included. The particular blindness of the culture warrior is that he permits himself to think God is pleased by coerced behavior; by requiring people to say "one nation, under God" even if they do not yet *believe* in God (which strikes me as an instance of taking the Lord's name in vain). The culture warrior's religion and his patriotism are in conflict. His Christianity teaches him that God is not pleased with mere external confession of insincere religious faith; but his patriotism just cannot accept the fact that his culture is moving in directions of which he disapproves. He desires to be proud of his nation; and he therefore concludes (wrongly, in my estimation) that it is better to have a public display of commitment to Christianity that is the result of coercion than to have a decline in the public display of commitment to Christianity.

Haven't we already had a historical experiment that is precisely what the culture warriors want? Wasn't ancient Israel a nation whose constitution demanded obedience to the revealed laws of God, and didn't its executive branch use coercion to attain such obedience? Did Israel not, effectively, have the Ten Commandments in its courthouse? Yet which prophet ever had anything good to say about the nation? Indeed, as Jesus and the apostles more bluntly put it, which of the prophets did they not kill? If theocracy didn't work in Israel, where God divinely *instituted* it, why do people insist on believing it will work in places where God manifestly has *not* instituted it?

Why These Are Failures

None of these false surrogates for real Christian proclamation nourishes the soul. They may inform or instruct about some aspects of religion, but they do not nourish *faith*; they do not feed *faith*. We feed on Christ himself, and we do so not by some physical eating of his body, but through faith in the Christ proclaimed in Word and sacrament.[15] These four alternatives have left much of the evangelical and Reformed

15. If you find this idea odd, don't take my word for it; read Wallace's *Calvin's Doctrine of the Word and Sacrament*, from which, in large measure, I derived the notion.

church malnourished. People know what they ought to do, but they are dispirited and lethargic, without the vision, drive, or impetus to live with and for Christ. And the reason for this dispirited condition is that the pulpit is largely silent about Christ. He is mentioned only as an afterthought or append-age to a sermon; in many churches, he is never proclaimed as the central point of a sermon, and surely not on a regular, weekly basis.

I have witnessed malnutrition of the physical sort this year, as I've already spent three months undergoing radia-tion and chemotherapy for a cancerous tumor in my diges-tive tract (and still have two surgeries and seven months of chemotherapy to look forward to). A little fellow to start with, I've lost thirty pounds. Many days while undergoing simultaneous radiation and chemotherapy treatments, my physical exhaustion was unlike anything I'd ever experienced. More than once, having settled back in the reclining chair to nap, I awakened without the strength even to sit up, and had to call my wife to stand behind the recliner and push it (and me) forward. Now, I wasn't a very good professor during this time. My morning classes were canceled so that I could be driven each weekday to Allegheny General Hospital for my radiation treatments; and I also missed a number of my afternoon classes because my fatigue or discomfort was simply too great to be able to stand in front of a class for an hour. How could I become a better professor? By trying harder? By reading a book on teaching? By introspecting about whether I really *am* a teacher? By listening to a diatribe about what's wrong with the educational system in our culture in recent decades? No; I simply needed *nourishment*. Until my digestive tract would handle food, and convert it into that which the body needs, nothing would make me a better teacher. And my physical malnourishment has reminded me of the spiritual malnourishment of the evangelical and Reformed churches—churches in which almost anything is preached other than the perfect fitness and competence of Christ to save to the uttermost those who come to God through him.

Do These Four Failures Have a Place?

I'm certainly not about to reverse face here and make a brief for preaching that fails in its basic content. But I sympathize with each of these failures in one sense (well, at least three of them; I have no attraction to the "how-to" heresy). There is a place in the overall ministry of the church for instruction in moral behavior. I myself, when pastoring, led my church in nine months of adult Sunday school study of the Westminster Larger Catechism's exposition of the Decalogue. There is also a place, especially in visitation and pastoral counseling, for challenging the complacent to examine whether they have truly rested in Christ. And there is a place for a theistic analysis of our culture. I myself have occasionally presented weekend conferences on that very theme, evaluating the distinctive traits of American culture and considering their compatibility with biblical values.

But the pulpit is almost never the place to do this. The pulpit is the place to declare the fitness of Christ's person, and the adequacy of both his humiliated and exalted work for sinners. If such proclamation sharpens moral vision, convicts the complacent, or creates in us dissatisfaction with our current culture, so be it. But these occur as occasional secondary results of Christ-centered preaching; they are not its purpose. Dabney's logic is irrefutable: there is a relation between what predominates in our preaching and what we deem to be of greatest importance. Some things in our preaching will occur with "a prominence suitable to their importance."[16] Along with Luther, Calvin, Dabney, and representatives from our own generation, I would suggest that nothing is more important for Christian proclamation than the central realities of the person, character, and work of Christ. When anything else predominates, the necessary inference of our hearers is that morality, or cultural improvement, or introspecting about our own spiritual health, is a more important consideration.

Curiously, when one considers the instructive role of the apostles in the early church, it is ironic that in many churches today, instruction has been handed over to the nonordained. Many ministers never teach regularly in the educational programs of their churches. As a result, the pulpit becomes their only occasion to inform people; and this is what causes some of them to fall prey to the four failures. In the nine years that

16. Robert Lewis Dabney, *Sacred Rhetoric: or a Course of Lectures on Preaching* (Edinburgh: Banner of Truth, 1979), 114.

I pastored, I taught almost every Sunday morning, and on many Tuesday evenings. Because of this, my sermons did not need to carry the entire weight of general Christian catechesis; they needed only to do what public Christian proclamation must do: declare Christ, and him crucified.

If preaching, in its authentic biblical, apostolic (and Reformational) sense, is to be recovered, it will also be necessary to recover an enduring commitment to Christ-centered, expository preaching, in addition to cultivating the necessary pre-ministerial sensibilities. Ministers will need to renounce their tendency to use the pulpit as a catchall, a place from which they attempt to do everything, and will need to return it to its proper place of proclaiming how (and how *well*) God reconciles himself to hopelessly lost sinners through the person and work of that beloved Son in whom he is well pleased.

A return to such Christ-centered preaching, however, probably cannot occur apart from cultivating the sensibility of reading texts closely (since it is the New Testament *texts* that teach us to preach Christ). And almost surely this change will not occur apart from cultivating a sensibility of the significant—because *only* a true sense of what is significant will cause a minister to realize that nothing in the entire history of human affairs is more significant than what the God-man has done; therefore, nothing should crowd the proclamation of Christ from the center of Christian preaching.

Johnny could preach, though he does so rarely now. Johnny is still made in God's image, and has latent sensibilities that can be cultivated in such a manner as to make him a competent preacher, even though our culture does not cultivate those sensibilities in its ordinary course of events. If Johnny loves his profession, loves his flock, and above all loves what Christ has so competently done for sinners, he will find sufficient motivation to cultivate those latent sensibilities, and participate in the return to our culture of a vigorous Christian pulpit. That Johnny would do so is the desire and prayer that undergirds every sentence in this book.

5

TEACHING JOHNNY
TO PREACH

ALL THAT HAS BEEN SAID to this point might leave the impression that the situation is hopeless. If I have left that impression, I have done so unwittingly and unintentionally, because I don't believe the situation is hopeless. The waves of church history have their crests and troughs, irregular though they may be. But the crests are not the result of the moon's gravitational pull or any other physical reality. They are the result of candid, honest self-criticism while in the troughs. At moments, the church or her leaders have undertaken honest self-criticism, and when such criticism reveals serious trouble, the church resolves with God's help to amend her ways.

Human sensibilities can be cultivated, either by the common activities of a particular culture or by the deliberate choice of individuals. If those who were preparing for the ministry (or those already in it) understood how profoundly different they are from people who lived even forty years ago, they could begin the process of cultivating those traits that our culture does not cultivate, by a deliberate and disciplined use of their own time. But the solution is not more books on homiletics (excellent ones have already been written and are available), nor is it to require more classes on homiletics at seminary.

The solution is to cultivate those pre-homiletical sensibilities that are necessary to preach well. If, by way of example, an illiterate but sincere Christian came to me and said he wanted to be a minister, and wanted to preach God's Word to others, I wouldn't initially send him to seminary. I'd encourage him to learn to read. How can he *preach* the Word of God if he can't *read* the Word of God? Similarly, reading texts closely is a skill—a skill distinct from reading generally or reading for information. Thus, many people today are illiterate in a particular way (illiterate of how to read texts closely), and they must devote themselves to acquiring this sensibility before they can be taught how to expound ancient, inspired texts.

Similarly, while many people can talk, not everyone has acquired the skill of carefully or thoughtfully *composed* speech; such people must first expend effort to develop this general capacity before they can learn to deliver a carefully composed speech about an ancient inspired text. And while people still have eyes and ears, these senses are less practiced than they once were at distinguishing the significant from the insignificant.[1] Following are some suggestions that, if followed, would have the natural consequence of producing better preachers.

Annual Review

I may as well get the most frightening one on the table first; the rest will then be comparatively easy. Most ministers will never know how bad their preaching really is without an annual review. They look out on Sunday morning, see a number of people present, and reason to themselves: "Well, I must be doing a pretty good job as a preacher because many people come to hear me." While this kind of conjecture is understandable, it is frequently wrong. Many people, myself included, consider it a Christian duty to attend the worship of God on the first day of the week. We do so (when not ill or otherwise prevented) every Sunday of our lives, whether our preacher is excellent or whether he is wretched. When we select a church to attend, we take a number of factors into account, including proximity, the theological stance of the church, the skill and character of the pastor, the skill and character of the elders and deacons, the Christian character of others present, and above all, the other local options. Sometimes one finds oneself in a location where

1. Television-watching prohibits such discernment. One simply cannot regard the significant as more important than the insignificant, and then plop himself in front of a television for two to three hours an evening. The only way the conscience can survive such a colossal waste of a human life is for the individual to refuse to *entertain* the question of the difference between the significant and the insignificant.

there is no church within a forty-five-minute drive that is agreeable in its theology and whose minister can preach. So one attends anyway, but not because of the minister; one attends in spite of the minister.

Thus, it will not do just to assume that one is doing a good job of preaching; some sort of review is necessary. I believe at least five or six of Robert Lewis Dabney's cardinal requisites outlined in chapter 1 can be tested by carefully designed survey questions. Some can be tested even more easily. Unity can be tested simply by calling several people at random on Tuesday or Wednesday and asking them what the sermon was about (better to have someone other than the pastor make this call). If, several days after the sermon, many or most hearers do not have any idea what it was about, or if they have *different* ideas, then the sermon plainly and manifestly failed at this crucial point. Other similar assessment surveys and forms are sometimes found in homiletical textbooks.

And if one finds this plan too frightening to consider, one could do a more general assessment, and simply take the primary ministerial tasks (preaching, counseling, pastoral visitation, teaching, administration, etc.), put them on a form, and ask members of the congregation to rank them in order of their perception of the minister's competence. One would think that every minister would aspire to find preaching at the top of the list, but I suspect few would find it so. Or you could simply ask ten or twelve people at random to submit to the session their thoughts on the minister's comparative abilities, and the session could review these assessments and provide a general summary for the minister's use.

Alternatively, a sermon or two could be submitted annually to presbytery for review (put numbers rather than names on them, and have some committee chairman assign the numbers, so that the matter remains discreet). That is, it is not logistically difficult to find some way of assessing preaching ability; the difficulty plainly resides in the fact that ministers are terrified that they will discover that they are failing. Just as a middle-aged man doesn't wish to ask his physician about his chest pains, for fear of what he might learn, the typical minister doesn't ask about his preaching competence for fear that he will discover that his preaching is not edifying to his hearers. Thus, while I don't consider it a moral necessity to conduct an annual review of the minister, I think, under the present circumstances, that it is about the only way for people to discover just how bad the situation has become.

Cultivating the Sensibility of Reading Texts Closely

As I mentioned above, I do not believe the present situation is hopeless, because I believe the human sensibilities can be shaped. Sensibilities that are absent today could be present in a year or two if an effort were made to cultivate them. This is the unstated assumption behind the 1940 Stone lectures given at Princeton Seminary by Charles Grosvenor

Osgood, later published under the title *Poetry as a Means of Grace.*[2] Osgood did not argue that poetry is a means of grace in the technical, theological sense; rather, he was giving lectures to seminarians on how to prepare for their profession, and his thesis was that the sensibilities necessary to preach well were best shaped by reading verse.

To fully appreciate these lectures, one must consider their historical circumstances. They were given over a decade *before* the flowering of commercial television. Thus, even before the culture had changed profoundly by replacing reading with television as the dominant cultural medium, Osgood believed the clergy would be more competent if they developed the habit of the close reading of texts by studying verse. One can only imagine what Osgood would say if he were alive today. One can reasonably assume, however, that he would have retained his belief that the human sensibilities can be cultivated; and if particular sensibilities are not being cultivated by the culture's dominant practices, they can still be cultivated by individuals who choose to live differently.

2. Princeton, NJ: Princeton University Press, 1942. Consider this gem from page 14: "Literature is strangely procreant. Vigor and grace beget vigor and grace. . . . A man in daily contact with say Johnson or Dante, or whoever his chosen seer may be, with their vigor, their wit, their imagery, their deep sense of the world's tragedy, their struggle to turn it to account in terms of beauty or truth or behavior, will inevitably catch from them something of their sense, their feeling, their intellectual and spiritual thrust, which is bound to assert itself in the quality of his own expression and his ministrations. It cannot be otherwise. In this deeper and subtler way the style of your speech grows stronger and purer under the influence of a great poet, while it becomes more distinctly and peculiarly your own." Osgood's is a marvelous, stimulating book, and it says volumes about the contemporary clergy that many of them have read Stephen Covey's *Seven Habits*, but almost none have read Osgood or the poets he recommends.

The present situation could certainly improve, and even improve dramatically. My thesis is merely that it will take a double perception to do so: a perception of how bad the present situation really is, and a perception of the sensibilities that must be developed to improve the situation. Assuming that this double perception or double vision can be attained, the situation is far from hopeless.

Before (or during, or after) seminary, the ministerial candidate can and should make efforts to cultivate the sensibilities requisite to preaching well. Perhaps the most straightforward way to do this is to follow the late James Montgomery Boice's example. When Boice left Stony Brook, Frank Gaebelein directed him to Harvard University to pursue a degree in English literature. It is no surprise, therefore, that one of the late twentieth century's most natural and competent expository preachers was Jim Boice. His pre-divinity training cultivated careful attentiveness to texts; he was a close, careful reader of texts long before he began his study of Greek, Hebrew, homiletics, or systematic theology. Some people are pleasantly surprised at how successful Boice's successor, Dr. Philip G. Ryken, has been. I tell them that they shouldn't be surprised: Ryken's father chaired the Department of English Literature at Wheaton College for many years. Philip Ryken was reared in an environment that took texts seriously, and he developed throughout his life those sensibilities that make one a good expositor, and therefore a potentially good expository preacher.

I still tell every incoming freshman at Grove City College who plans to major in religion (the department in which I teach) that if he intends to go to divinity school and become a minister, he should *not* major in religion but in English literature. None of them listen to me, of course, and I get the most puzzled looks from them (and looks of consternation from my departmental colleagues), but I continue to make the effort, even though it never succeeds. I think on occasion I have at least succeeded in getting an individual or two to minor in English literature, so I will continue the largely ineffectual effort.[3]

Formal study of English literature, however, is not necessary. Informally, one can learn to read poetry by reading books about how to read poetry, and by reading classic defenses of verse (such as those by Spenser and Shelley, or the life-changing *An Experiment in Criticism*, by C. S. Lewis) or essays on poetic theory and criticism, while also reading anthologies of poetry.[4] I do not recommend, ordinarily, that one devote the majority of his attention to post–World War II poetry; from then on, poetry took on an almost perversely iconoclastic character, as though the severest obscurity were the highest attainment. While such verse demands a close reading, it also frustrates all but the most

3. Nor is my advice on this point idiosyncratic. When I was still in high school, and wrestling with the early evidence of a call to the Christian ministry, my own pastor, the Rev. Robert F. Cochran, advised that I pursue a general liberal-arts education, with a heavy emphasis on English literature, concurring in the advice that Gaebelein gave to Boice.

4. Such as the recently published *The Best Poems of the English Language: From Chaucer Through Robert Frost*, ed. Harold Bloom (New York: HarperCollins, 2004). What a terrific book this is, containing not only a single-volume anthology of important English verse, but introductory essays and interspersed commentary and essays by the American dean of literary criticism.

devoted readers, and does not always reward close reading in the way that earlier verse did.

Cultivating the Sensibility of Composed Communication

Those who are preparing for the ministry should also write handwritten letters whenever there is justification for doing so (just yesterday, I wrote one to a mechanic who worked on our car last week). The handwritten letter requires composition: that one consider before one writes what one wishes to say, and how one wishes to say it. There is no "delete" key, and there are no emoticons to compensate for lack of clarity. One must say what one wishes to say clearly, so that the reader understands on the first reading.

For those already in the ministry, it is well to keep some personal letterhead on hand when one prays for his congregation throughout the week. Often, while praying, one will get an inclination to write a brief personal note. Not only is the writing of these notes an encouragement in itself to those who receive them, it cultivates in the minister the habit of thoughtful composition, which will ultimately spill over into sermons.

In addition to letters, ministers should compose other material: articles for theological, religious, or denominational periodicals; editorials for magazines or newspapers; journal entries; anything. And note that I think it matters not at all whether any of these ever get published. The value resides in the shaping of one's sensibilities and abilities (especially that of composition) that comes from organizing one's thoughts into writing. Many readers of this book, for instance, may be surprised to learn that Samuel Miller, who began teaching at Princeton Seminary in its second year (1813), recommended that ministers write prayers devotionally. In his *Thoughts on Public Prayer*, Miller argued that the practice of composing and writing prayers privately would inevitably influence the nature of one's public prayers for the better. I believe he was unquestionably right. Not only was Miller right, but he was right even for his generation (mid-nineteenth century). If members of a generation that antedated any of the electronic media by over fifty years could become more competent in their public leading of worship through composition, how much more would this be true today, in a culture overwhelmed by what Todd Gitlin calls a "torrent of sounds and images."

Most pre-ministerial candidates, and most ministers, would be well served by taking a nonreligious course on public speaking. Once religious texts are involved, too many complicating factors enter the picture. One might wonder whether the Holy Spirit was "leading" him to a particular insight in the text, or a particular way of organizing the sermon or applying it. One might slip into certain habits that one has unconsciously observed in other ministers (since humans have profound imitative capacities). In a nonreligious setting, however, these complications are absent, and one can learn the important distinction between good and poor organization, clarity versus obscurity, specific language versus general language, and so on.

One might even consider joining Rotary International. I know several ministers who have been Rotarians for years, and they profess to learn a good deal about organized public speaking by listening to the speakers at Rotary. Rotarians have the obvious advantage, as public speakers, of never deceiving themselves into thinking the Holy Spirit "led" them to outline their speech as they did; they accept responsibility for the organizational choices they make while preparing their talks, and they therefore almost always make better choices than ministers do.

Some ministers work on the technical aspects of their sermon preparation by developing a homiletical partner: another minister with whom they meet once or twice a month to discuss their recent sermons, and why they constructed them as they did. The feedback of another set of eyes can be very helpful, and this process is a great aid in developing the sensibility of thoughtful composition. Conversing about potentially different ways of organizing the same material makes one increasingly aware of compositional choices.

Cultivating Pre-Homiletical Sensibilities: Johnny Can Learn to Preach

Other methods for cultivating one's pre-homiletical sensibilities could be suggested, and it is not my purpose to do anything here other than to offer some beginning suggestions.[5] But it is necessary to repeat here that human sensibilities can be cultivated; the person who does not care for Johannes Brahms today can, within several months or years, cultivate a sensibility to appreciate the formal perfection and the remarkably restrained passion of his music. The person who today cannot read a Shakespearean sonnet with pleasure or understanding can learn, in several months or years, to do so with both.[6] To preach the Word of God well, one must already have cultivated, at a minimum, three sensibilities: the sensibility of the close reading of texts, the sensibility of composed communication, and the sensibility of the significant. Without these, a person simply cannot preach, any more than he could if his larynx were removed or he were utterly illiterate. But our present culture does not cultivate any one of these sensibilities, and pre-ministerial candidates, or ministers themselves, must undertake their cultivation if preaching is to be rescued from its present moribund state.

While most of my thoughts are addressed to ministers and pre-ministerial candidates, congregations should not overlook their responsibility in the matter. As long as the typical congregation runs its minister ragged with clerical, administrative,

5. I am considering writing a sequel to this book, titled *Feed My Sheep*, which would devote itself more thoroughly to providing advice on how to cultivate appropriate pre-homiletical sensibilities.

6. Aided, in this case, by the wonderful introduction by Helen Vendler, *The Art of Shakespeare's Sonnets* (Cambridge: The Belknap Press of Harvard University Press, 1997). Professor Vendler had the remarkable advantage of being reared in a home where her mother had memorized all 154 of the sonnets, and whose recitation of them around the home undoubtedly contributed substantially to Professor Vendler's own sensibilities as a Shakespeare scholar.

and other duties; and as long as such a congregation expects the minister to be out five or six nights a week visiting or at meetings, the minister will not have time in his schedule to read, write, or reflect. In short, those sensibilities essential to effective preaching will remain uncultivated.

Dr. Kenneth Swetland, from Gordon-Conwell, recommended a good practice for our students when they were candidating for church positions: that in the later stages of that process, whenever possible, the candidate meet with the appropriate committee and, with a chalkboard or whiteboard, ask the committee members what they expected a minister to do. Dr. Swetland recommended that after listing the variety of activities on the board, the candidate then ask the committee how much time it would take to perform these tasks, including the preparation time. Ordinarily, the result of this exercise is that the committee realizes that the minister is expected to work about seventy-five hours a week, and also to be a good example of a family man! Churches cannot continue to exact such a toll from their ministers while expecting them to preach well, because preaching well requires more than preparing sermons; it requires preparing *oneself* as the kind of human who has the sensibilities prerequisite to preaching. An individual without time to read broadly and intensely, without time to reflect on life, without time to compose (even if merely in a personal journal), is not likely to be an individual who can preach.

Johnny is still fearfully and wonderfully made in God's image; and any particular Johnny could develop those sensibilities necessary to being a competent preacher. Our culture, at this moment, will not develop those sensibilities, and so Johnny will cultivate them only if he makes some self-conscious and deliberately countercultural choices about how he wishes his sensibilities to be shaped. My hope and prayer in writing this brief volume is that some will accept that responsibility, and begin or continue the process of shaping those sensibilities requisite to preaching well.

War of Words
Paul David Tripp

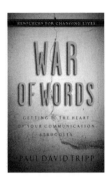

$14.99 paper, 280 pages
ISBN 978-0-87552-604-1

"An important and biblical book about God and words. We all talk, but very few of us really think about our words—the power, the blessing, the gift, the effect, and the danger of words. This book will make you think, it will make you think before you speak, and, best of all, it will make you think of *Him* before you speak. Read it. You'll be glad." —STEVE BROWN

"As you read this book, you become aware of the fact that Paul Tripp knows his Bible and he knows people. . . . I will certainly recommend it to my students, counselees, and friends." —WAYNE MACK

"Reading this book was like taking a bath in encouragement and insight from which I'm still dripping wet. It gave me ideas for a dozen evenings of devotions with my teenagers." —STEVE ESTES

Sermons That Shaped America
WILLIAM S. BARKER AND SAMUEL T. LOGAN JR.

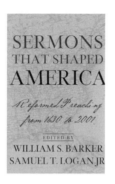

$19.99 paper, 464 pages
ISBN 978-0-87552-003-2

An anthology of 18 sermons preached in American pulpits between 1630 and 2001, from Cotton to Keller. These sermons possess historical significance and spiritual power.

"These messages are presented as trustworthy guides to the various kinds of faithfulness required to transform a nation. Such guidance serves to provide fresh courage and confidence for the unique, and sometime lonely, paths God calls his preachers to walk today." —BRYAN CHAPELL

"The sermons in this volume, which span the decades between America's beginning and its shattering September 2001, confirm that the Word of God, preached boldly and with high pertinence, . . . has a supreme influence explained only by the power of Christ Jesus." —JOEL NEDERHOOD

20 Controversies That Almost Killed a Church
Richard L. Ganz

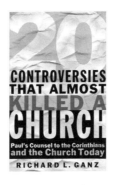

$12.99 paper, 240 pages
ISBN 978-0-87552-790-1

Revisits the controversies that threatened the Corinthian church, enabling us to see both the snares to avoid and the goal of godliness to be pursued.

"A helpful and interesting exposition of 1 Corinthians. Rather than a verse-by-verse commentary, the volume offers a discussion of major themes. That Richard Ganz has sprinkled these discussions with examples from his own ministry further enhances it. Thoroughly biblical." —Jay Adams

"Richard Ganz has escorted our common rabbi, St. Paul, to the microphone so his first letter to the Corinthians can be heard afresh by a generation that needs his message as much as, if not more than, did the original recipients." —Steve Schlissel

T. David Gordon (MAR, ThM, Westminster Theological Seminary; PhD, Union Theological Seminary in Virginia) is professor of religion and Greek at Grove City College, where since 1999 he has taught courses in religion, Greek, humanities, and media ecology. Prior to that, he taught New Testament (primarily Pauline studies) for thirteen years at Gordon-Conwell Theological Seminary, and for nine years he was pastor of Christ Presbyterian Church in Nashua, New Hampshire.

Dr. Gordon has contributed to a number of books and study Bibles (his notes on John's gospel appear in the *New Geneva Study Bible* and the *Reformation Study Bible*) and has published scholarly reviews and articles in journals such as *New Testament Studies, The Westminster Theological Journal, Interpretation,* and *Journal for the Evangelical Theological Society.* His popular articles have appeared in periodicals such as *Modern Reformation, Tabletalk, Decision,* and *Lay Leadership.*

With his wife Dianne he attends Grace Anglican Church in Slippery Rock, Pennsylvania.